The Victorians
At Home And At Work

Hilary and Mary Evans

The Victorians
At Home And At Work

AS ILLUSTRATED BY THEMSELVES

ARCO PUBLISHING COMPANY, INC.
New York

Published by Arco Publishing Company, Inc.
219 Park Avenue South, New York, N.Y. 10003

Copyright © 1973 by Hilary and Mary Evans

Library of Congress Catalog Card Number 72-94234

ISBN 0-668-02914-5

Printed in Great Britain

Contents

*All the illustrations in this book are from the
Mary Evans Picture Library*

Detail from LONDON IN 1862
(William M'Connell *Leisure Hour* 1862)

Chapter One

Victorian People

THIS book is about the Victorians: which means it is about the people of Britain, of every social class, who made up one of the most complex societies in history, at a moment in time when that society was developing more rapidly than ever before—economically, technologically, socially and culturally. To treat such a society as a single entity would be hard enough in any case; it is made harder still by the accident that the queen who gave the age her name reigned for more than sixty years. Our Victorians span three generations, during which they almost doubled in number: Victoria ruled over twice as many subjects in the last year of her life as when she first came to the throne, not counting the millions of her Empire subjects who gave her their less immediate allegiance.

The first generation of Victorians, the ones who somewhat unenthusiastically welcomed Victoria to her throne in 1837, lived in a world where the social structure had scarcely altered since the 18th century; where easy travel was still a novelty, and most trade and industry were conducted on a local level; where such concepts as education and free libraries for all, health services and pensions for all, holidays and unemployment pay for all were hardly dreamt of, let alone implemented; where workmen were not allowed to unite to protect their interests though their employers could and did; where women and children could be hideously exploited in mines and factories without interference from outside; where news could not travel from one part of the world to another any faster than a man could carry it. And because all these things help to shape the way people think, those early Victorians thought in radically different ways from their no less Victorian grandchildren.

So allowance must be made for the time factor; it must also be made for the myth factor. The Victorians created, for their own amusement, a fantasy version of their own world. We find it exemplified most obviously in their novels and magazine fiction, in the cartoons of *Punch* and *Judy* and *Fun*, in all forms of ephemera from greetings cards to the Christmas supplements and Almanacks. Even Charles Dickens, for all his awareness of the bitter realities of Victorian life, was sufficiently a child of his age to be

7

trapped into reinforcing its sentimental self-portrait. It is temptingly easy to be diverted from our pursuit of the real Victorians and to accept this beguiling alternative: indeed, so all-pervasive is the myth that it is almost impossible to avoid accepting some of it as fact, giving the Victorians a reputation for 'softness' which they hardly deserve.

There is a third factor which we must take into account: the development in communication, the most significant of all the material changes which transformed the Victorian scene. Rapid communication means rapid dissemination of ideas—and the flow of ideas erodes differences between people and communities. Compared with ourselves, the Victorians travelled seldom and slowly. As a consequence, differences between them remained wide, and we should always hesitate before assenting to any easy generalisations about them. Do we think of the archetypal Victorians as conservative? Yet theirs was the great age of radical reform—the history of the age was punctuated by riots every few years, and even the future Edward VII had to declare 'We are all socialists nowadays!' Do we think of them as insular? Throughout the world there were Britons trading, fighting, exploring, building, or simply travelling for curiosity's sake. Do we think of them as narrow-minded? Their imagination spurred them to break out of old-fashioned dogma in almost every sphere of knowledge. Do we think of them as unquestioningly devout? The atheism to which many of them subscribed was a fiercer brand than any preached today. Do we think of them as conventional? Beneath the

THE MOB PULLING DOWN THE RAILINGS IN PARK LANE
(*Illustrated London News* 1866)

8

TRAVELLING IN THE EGYPTIAN DESERT
(*Illustrated London News* 1857)

custom-ridden surface of Victorian life they did their own thing with greater assurance than the hesitant generations which followed them.

Does all this mean that it is absurd to try to present a composite picture of the Victorians? No, because underlying these differences and variations we find shared characteristics, values and attitudes, which were common to the majority of British people during this period. Slice them wherever you like, the Victorians were still and always Victorians.

We think of the Victorians as contented and self-satisfied—but when they felt strongly, they were ready to express their feelings violently. When in 1866 the police sought to prevent the Reform League from holding a meeting in Hyde Park, a London mob tore down the railings. Such revolutionary action seemed to bring results: certainly it was only a few months later that a Conservative government pushed through the Second Reform Bill.

Though travel was infinitely more difficult, uncomfortable, dangerous, time-consuming and costly than it is today, the Victorians were not deterred. They sailed the Atlantic in open boats, made long cross-country flights in open balloons, climbed hitherto unconquered mountains, crossed uncharted deserts and penetrated unmapped jungles, with none of the sophisticated equipment the 20th century adventurer takes for granted.

The Victorians' thirst for knowledge manifested itself in many different ways—in the great number of popular scientific journals and text books which were published, in the scientific societies and working men's institutes which sprang up in almost every town, as well as in the private ventures of individuals, more often amateur than professional.

9

Many valuable discoveries were made by private people pursuing their own particular hobby-horses in their own way.

The majority of Victorians were more or less devout church-goers; but the free-thinkers were outspoken, and ready to stand by their non-beliefs. Bradlaugh was expelled from the House of Commons in 1881 for refusing to take the requisite Christian oath; his constituents—many of whom must themselves have been believers—backed him up, and he was repeatedly re-elected, only to be expelled every time. Finally in 1886 he was permitted to retain both his seat and his principles.

CHARLES BRADLAUGH EXPELLED FROM THE COMMONS
(*Graphic* 1881)

We think of the Victorians as prudish, yet in many respects their attitude to moral matters was closer to the open frankness of the 18th century or the Regency than to the self-conscious 'modesty' of subsequent generations. To take just one example: nude bathing was regarded as normal throughout most of Victoria's reign, certainly for children, often for men and even occasionally for women.

BOYS BATHING
(From a drawing by H. R. Robertson *Art Journal* 1873)

ARRIVAL OF ARISTOCRATS AT COUNTRY SEAT
(George du Murier in *The Graphic* 1888)

A Victorian aristocrat returns home—and an army of paid retainers turns out in force to greet him. The senior servants are rewarded with personal attention—the butler and the estate manager, first, while the housekeeper hovers expectantly on the steps. Behind her are the footmen and maids, cook and her staff; while to one side are the gardeners, farmworkers and other estate personnel. The cost of maintaining such an establishment was of course prodigious; fortunately for them, the elegant tip of the aristocratic iceberg frequently rested on a solid foundation of unsightly but highly rewarding mines and mills.

THE ARISTOCRACY

Matthew Arnold, probably the most perceptive analyst of the Victorian social structure, reflected, 'One has often wondered whether upon the whole earth there is anything so unintelligent, so unapt to perceive how the world is really going, as an ordinary young Englishman of our upper class.' However we account for this refusal or inability to perceive—whether or not we attribute it to a failure of nerve among the descendants of the former ruling class—the shift in power from the aristocracy is basic to any assessment of the Victorian age.

In the early Victorian period the aristocracy and the rich were largely the same people. They were often unimaginably rich. When we hear of an aristocrat like the first Earl of Durham saying he considered £40,000 per annum 'a moderate income—such a one as a man might jog along with'—and when we translate that sum into a real buying-power of at least £200,000 (and virtually tax-free into the bargain), we are liable to be indignant if not positively disgusted. But the majority of Victorians were still ready to acquiesce in such inequality. The aristocrat himself inherited without question the values of his forefathers along with their estates, genuinely believing that he was in

VISCOUNTESS POWERSCOURT
(Portrait by J. Ross engraved by W. H. Mote
c1840)

LORD SOUTHAMPTON
(Drawing by J. Grant engraved
Andrew Duncan c1840)

some way superior to the great majority of his fellow-countrymen; and only a small minority of those fellow-countrymen questioned this belief. Even if he felt conscience-bound to justify his own existence (in the sight of God, that is—to the opinion of his fellow-countrymen he was generally indifferent) by some service to the community, he nevertheless expected the community to repay his services by continuing to maintain him in a quite disproportionate degree of comfort.

Such a man would ride out from his elegant country seat or town house on a weekday morning, without troubling his mind that at the same moment thousands of his ill-fed ill-housed ill-dressed ill-educated fellow-creatures were sweating in mine and mill, and would do so for sixteen hours a day, six days a week, earning him the money to maintain his stables and the rest of his establishment. For every Shaftesbury who forced his Factory Act on an unwilling Parliament, or Coke who devoted his energies to revolutionising farming, there were thousands who contributed infinitely less to the community than they took out of it, and whose lives were geared to an artificial annual cycle of full-time leisure where the seasons were the shooting season, the hunting season and—to placate his wife and daughters—the London season (at a time of year when there was nothing to hunt or shoot in any case).

Arnold called them 'Barbarians' because, for all their fine breeding and gentlemanly tastes, they had learned nothing about their proper role in the community, were aware of their privileges but not of their responsibilities. And ultimately it was this failure to collaborate in the national effort which destroyed them. At the beginning of Victoria's reign they ruled the nation: at the end of it, their power was hardly more significant than that of the monarch herself.

LORD BRAYE
(Lithograph 1880s)

LADY MABEL BRUDENELL-BRUCE
(Lithograph 1880s)

ARISTOCRATIC TYPES

At the start of the Victorian era, the female of the species might pay lip-service to culture, if only to the extent of being portrayed with a book in her hand: by the latter end of the reign she had frankly reduced her interests to the social and sporting. As for her male counterpart, early Victorian or late, he was far more likely to be at home on the hunting field or covert than anywhere else.

THE MEN HUNCHED THEIR SHOULDERS AND STOOPED THEIR HEADS
(G. G. Kilburne in *Cassell's Family Magazine* 1882)

THE MIDDLE CLASSES

The middle classes were the great success story of the Victorian age. At their worst they were small-minded, dull, hypocritical, smug, tasteless, insular, bigoted, blinkered from all considerations except that of business; everything, in fact, that we most dislike about the period. But at their best, it was they who made the age what it was. They may not have been numerically the majority, but it was their strength which gave the Victorian community its backbone. It was they who demanded the right to elect the nation's leaders—and they who told the leaders what to do. They created the conventions of the age—and followed them. They forged its values—and lived by them.

They caused the railways and the bridges, the tarred roads and the canals to be constructed. They discovered natural selection and the geological foundations of pre-history. They traced the source of the Nile and unearthed the stones of Nineveh. They built the factories and the stores, the town halls and the art galleries. And because they were the heirs of Cromwell's puritan commonwealth, they inherited a puritan conscience which spurred them to legislate for better working and living conditions for all the community—and even for strangers outside it—against their own immediate personal interests. (It was calculated, for example, that the abolition of slavery cost British businessmen £20,000,000—equivalent to at least five times that sum today.) They found a nation where the only safeguards of life and liberty were the personal inclinations of autocratic lords and despotic factory-owners; they left a nation where those safeguards were written into the law of the land. In real terms, they achieved more than Magna Carta.

MANUFACTURER, FOREMAN AND WORKMEN IN A GUTTA-PERCHA FACTORY
(*The Illustrated Exhibitor* 1851)

SHE WHO MUST BE OBEYED

THE BREAD WINNER

MASTER GEORGE

THE DAUGHTER OF THE HOUSE

A HIGHLY RESPECTABLE FAMILY
(*Cassell's Family Magazine* 1893)

They did not manage to do everything. The British social structure when Victoria died was still an ill-balanced, unwieldy, convention-ridden edifice, hardly more than a prototype for the truly just society. But despite the changes and stresses which assailed it, it survived and functioned tolerably well—better, in any case, than that of most other nations. And so it became the exemplar not only for our own society today, but also for others throughout the world.

All this the Victorian middle classes achieved, but not without loss. Their victories were won only by neglecting many of the civilised elements in life. It is not without reason that we think of them as bigoted, hypocritical, blinkered; not for nothing that the French sneered at them as sacrificing everything to business and living by the motto 'Time is money'; not without cause that Matthew Arnold, middle class himself, labelled them 'Philistines'.

THE WORKING CLASSES

Today we can speak of 'the working class' with some degree of meaningfulness—there is a body of people, possessing a measure of cohesion, about whom the term can usefully be employed. In Victorian times this was hardly so. The populace was an amorphous mass, unaware of its identity, which had to be told by others that it existed at all.

NAVVIES AT WORK IN A RAILWAY CUTTING
(*Pearl of Days* 1884)

VIEW OF A DUST YARD
(Mayhew's *London Labour and the London Poor*)

If the rise of the middle class was the great success story of the age, its great failure was its inability to prevent the formation of a working class which considered that its interests were directly opposed to those of the other classes. The change in the social order which wrested the power from the aristocracy should have bound the other strata of society together in a common purpose; but this did not happen, and the age as a whole endorsed what was merely a new version of the old feudal baron/serf relationship, but with a new resentment built into it because the superior status of the middle-class employer was so very evidently *not* of divine origin. The very fact that the label 'working' was reserved for the lower class of workers is symptomatic of the tragic misunderstanding—the cleavage between 'them' and 'us' which was to grow wider as the age wore on, wider still in the age which followed.

Nevertheless, uneasy partnership as it was, it accomplished much. The British workman made real the vision of the middle-class entrepreneur. He sliced his canals and railway cuttings through the British landscape. He spanned the rivers with bridges and pierced the hills with tunnels. He drove the locomotives and sailed the ships, he delivered Rowland Hill's Penny Post and patrolled the streets in Peel's blue uniform, he farmed the land and marketed its produce, he served his superiors in home and office, and above all he and his wife and children operated the machines which in factory and mill up and down the country created the wealth which was the foundation of his country's greatness.

In return his country treated him appallingly. If he worked the land, he lived in a rural slum: if he worked in mill or mine, he lived in an urban slum. When Engels studied life in the factory towns of England in 1844, he concluded that this race 'must

17

A MANCHESTER COTTON FACTORY—DINNER TIME
(Charles Green *Graphic* 1872)

really have reached the lowest stage of humanity'. Who, reading the ghastly facts, could disagree?

That the working class survived at all was due not to its own efforts, but to those of a minority of its 'betters', assisted by the reluctant consciences of the rest. At the beginning of Victoria's reign it was believed that enlightened self-interest could be relied on to maintain the just equilibrium of society, but the stresses inflicted on the social structure by the industrial revolution proved such theories inadequate. Reluctantly, Britain had to realise that man-made laws, not the spontaneous operations of divinely constituted Nature, could alone ensure that everyone in society got his deserts. And so, Act by creaking Act, the working man was provided with some degree of protection against the growing pains of a society striving towards adulthood.

But there were some who were not prepared to wait, some who found older laws—or loopholes between laws—and exploited them for their own ends: the criminals, the demi-monde—'those who cannot or will not work' from Mayhew's penetrating survey of London's poor—those who were too impatient with the slow advance of progress to move obediently from square to square across the board. Then as now there were the smart boys and girls who successfully landed on the ladders, then as now the drop-outs who encountered only the snakes. In London's Rookeries, or walking the pavements of the Haymarket beneath the flaring gas-lamps, or sleeping beneath the arches of the Thames bridges and periodically jumping from their parapets, these too added their texture to the complex fabric of Victorian life: these too are Victorians.

SHARED VALUES

Such a diversity of creatures might seem to defy generalisation. And yet there were values which they shared in common, which gave them a unity deeper than all their differences.

Confidence—in themselves, in their country, in their way of life—was a quality shared by Victorians of all walks of life. They believed in themselves, they were willing to gamble on their own efforts. There were many more self-employed than today, far fewer who worked for others. And though this individualism was frequently inefficient, and eventually failed to withstand the tougher economic pressures of the 20th century, it stimulated qualities in the individual which were generally admirable if not always attractive.

We can see this exemplified in the popular attitude to the Queen. Towards the close of her reign she was loved and lauded, but during the earlier decades she was lampooned and ridiculed far more virulently than our sovereigns today—first because she was widely thought of as German, a feeling not helped by her marriage to a prince from Saxe-Coburg-Gotha, and secondly when, after Albert's early death, it was felt she was shirking her responsibilities. Because the Victorian expected a lot from himself, he expected a lot from others. He never forgot that he had put his monarch on her throne and he could take her off again: he expected a fair day's work from her as from any other paid employee.

The least attractive side of his self-confidence was his self-satisfaction. The Victorian could see that his country was successful where other nations were not. He watched the revolutions of 1848 throughout Europe, the civil wars of Italy and Spain, France and Portugal, Belgium and America, the neighbourly wars of Germany and Denmark and Austria and France; how could he help pitying, and so despising, even these so-called civilised countries, to say nothing of savage lands farther afield?

When his own country went to war—which he believed she did only in the best of causes—she invariably won. When she confined her efforts to commerce, she was even more spectacularly successful—in 1870 Britain's external trade was greater than that of France, Germany and Italy *together*, and three times that of the United States.

In almost every field of activity, from the building of railways to the mounting of exhibitions, from the opening up of unknown regions to the spreading of the Word of God, his country took the lead. That there might be faults and deficiencies in the structure of the machine, he was not so conceited as to doubt—but why tamper with a machine which was demonstrably working better than any other on show? Time enough to do that if the machine broke down, or someone else invented a better one.

It is easy enough, in retrospect, to sneer. The faults are so much plainer to see today.

But let us not forget the physical limitations of the age. We blame the Victorians, for example, for their ruthless colonialism, and with reason; but we must not forget that many of the operations we condemn were carried out thousands of miles from the responsible leadership back home, and that news of them took weeks, not seconds, to travel. Under such circumstances, what is more to be wondered at is the fact that, in the face of a lack of communication which we today can hardly conceive, many Victorians *did* challenge the morality of their imperialism, *did* question the actions of their emissaries in far-off lands.

For above all, for good or ill, the Victorians were sincere. If they made mistakes, it was seldom with evil intent. They believed that it is better to be a success than a failure, better to be rich than poor; but they also believed that it is better to be kind than harsh, better to be honest than dishonest, better to be just than unjust.

This book can show only a few facets of the life of the Victorians. Those facets have been chosen to illustrate as enlighteningly as possible how the beliefs of the Victorians were expressed in the way they lived, at home, at work, at play; in the way they built and furnished their homes, designed and equipped their cities; in their attitudes to education, government, religious observance, sexual behaviour; and above all in their social attitudes and inter-personal stances. In all these spheres, the Victorians evolved patterns which add up to create a unique life-style. By examining the component parts, we can hope to re-create the whole; and thus we can seek to form a balanced picture of the unique way of life created by these remarkable people.

For they really were remarkable. Remarkable because they were genuinely a society of people working for themselves, not to instructions from a few superiors. Remarkable because their efforts were directed into all spheres of activity, not just one here and one there. Remarkable because they combined—they *had* to combine—the art of reconstructing the social fabric along with the business of changing its component parts, like rebuilding a railway locomotive while it is travelling. Because the Victorians were faced with so vast and so complex a problem, they deserve our sympathy; because they succeeded in solving it as well as they did, they earn our admiration.

Chapter Two

The Victorians At Home

WHEN Victoria came to the throne, only about a quarter of her subjects lived in towns with more than 20,000 inhabitants, yet Britain was already irrevocably committed to becoming a primarily urban, industrialised society. The change was steady but rapid. On the one hand, country people continued to migrate to the towns; on the other, the towns spread farther and farther into the country, swallowing up fields and farms, turning villages into suburbs.

About 1870, the point of balance was reached. After that, the majority of people spent the greater part of their lives among streets rather than fields. Necessarily they had to fashion their way of life accordingly, matching it to all that urban life entails, whether for gain or loss: greater interdependence among neighbours but less individual self-sufficiency; wider choice of work and leisure activities but less space for them; greater flexibility in behaviour patterns but less scope for personal expression; greater involvement in public affairs but less freedom for private ones.

Moreover, apart from these obvious changes which living in a town imposes on a way of life, there was one very important additional difference. Those who went on living in the country continued to follow more or less traditional patterns of existence, whereas in the towns, new patterns had to be contrived to meet a new situation. Consequently it is the urban rather than the rural household which most truly exemplifies the characteristic Victorian way of life.

Town or country, however, it was the home which gave each way of life its focus. Be it never so squalid, the Victorians professed to believe that East or West, Home was Best. A middle-class ideal—but this was a period when middle-class standards set the pace. The Queen herself provided the example. Whether at her Highland home at Balmoral, her marine home at Osborne or her more formal homes at Windsor and Buckingham Palace, she presented a model for all to see of a respectable family life centred on the hearth. The domestic arts flourished as never before. Periodicals were entitled *Home Friend, Home Words, Cassell's Family Magazine, Sunday at Home.* Isabella Beeton was just one of many professional guides to the intricacies of house-

21

keeping. Even the reformers recognised that the first step towards ensuring that people lived decent lives was to ensure that they had decent homes to live them in. No survey of Victorian life can do otherwise than take the home as its starting point.

The prime maintainers of the traditional ways were of course the landed gentry who inhabited the topmost branches of the social tree. Every country district had its own leading family, living in 'the big house' which it had perhaps inhabited for generations. In these stately homes, life could take a variety of forms according to temperament and circumstances. The greatest of them, houses like Chatsworth, Hatfield or Blenheim, were veritable palaces. Their corridors were corridors of power, and life within their walls was hardly less formalised and regulated than that of a royal court. Armies of servants, with an elaborate hierarchical structure of their own, waited on the household and their guests.

Whether the family chose to devote themselves to political intrigue and public service, or were content to follow the gentlemanly pursuits of hunting and shooting, their country estate provided them with a superbly run base of operations. If they wished, they could amuse themselves by taking a prominent part in local affairs, exercising an almost divinely bestowed right to dominate the social structure of the neighbourhood. Or if they preferred, they could pass their lives insulated from all contact with the lesser mortality which dwelt outside the lodge gates.

Even on the landed gentry, the more sophisticated life of the towns exerted its pull. Just as in earlier ages the great lords had felt the necessity of maintaining a London

HUNT BREAKFAST
(George du Maurier in *Punch* 1889)

BELGRAVE SQUARE
(Cassell's *Old and New London* c1870)

establishment in order to be conveniently close to Court, so now all who claimed to be 'in Society' felt the need to spend at least part of the year—'the Season'—in Town. Their new town homes could not rival the magnificence of the great houses of Somerset, Arundel or Northumberland, which in Tudor days ran down from the Strand to the Thames, but they boasted their own share of splendour. In the fashionable squares of Mayfair and Belgravia, the great families of England lived as graciously as, if less spaciously than, they did in their country homes. But only from April to July. During the rest of the year, while the family were in the country, the blinds were drawn, only a caretaker in the basement kept guard. If a member of the family had to come up to town, the husband would put up at his club, his wife at a hotel, rather than go to the trouble of opening up their own house!

Life, for the exclusive few who participated in the Season, was a continual succession of garden parties and balls, shopping excursions and theatre visits, interspersed with the paying and receiving of social calls. Day after day the programme comprised little more than getting ready for the day's engagements—fulfilling them—and then recovering from them. As an occasional sop to their consciences, the members of the 'Haut Ton' might organise a Charity Bazaar or attend a ball in aid of some selected group of less fortunate mortals lower down the social ladder; but for the most part they enjoyed without question the leisure and pleasures to which their rank and fortune admitted them.

However, the aristocrats no longer possessed a monopoly of gracious living. In the

ARRIVING AT A SMART BALL, LONDON
(George du Maurier *Harper's Magazine* 1886)

A FIVE O'CLOCK TEA
(From a painting by J. L. Stewart *Magazine of Art* 1884)

country, it was true, only the wealthiest bankers could set themselves up as landlords beside the established lords, as Rothschild did at Waddesdon. But in town it was a different matter. Here the nouveaux riches from all walks of life—successful doctors, successful lawyers, successful railway entrepreneurs, even successful swindlers—could set up establishments to rival those of their titled neighbours. Successful artists like Millais and Leighton enjoyed rewards which enabled them to take their own place in society, instead—as in most ages before or since—of forming part of the entourage of others.

WADDESDON MANOR, NEAR AYLESBURY—HOME OF
THE BANKER BARON ROTHSCHILD
(*Illustrated London News* 1889)

MILLAIS' HOME, PALACE GATE, LONDON
(*Illustrated London News* 1896)

25

The new inhabitants of the towns lived where best they could. The impecunious crowded into lodging-houses; the well-to-do built houses for themselves or bought or rented houses that already existed. These latter took the form, as often as not, of those characteristic square-fronted Georgian terrace houses, each a simple unit in a functional whole, which offered a highly economical combination of maximum interior space with minimum street frontage. The box-shaped rooms within could be allocated in a variety of ways to suit individual needs. Today we can appreciate both the practical merits and the functional elegance of the design: the Victorians took the design for granted and were blind to the elegance. They dreamt of something nicer.

That 'something nicer' could take any number of forms. One alternative was offered by the villages which were being swallowed up by the spreading towns: old village houses found themselves transformed into suburban dwellings. They offered the additional advantage that their owner could cherish the illusion of living in the elegance of a former period—for then as now, there were many who looked back to the preceding age as one of gracious charm. Alas, what more often happened was that the old village houses were pulled down to make room for a grander replacement.

Those who could afford to, built houses for themselves. A successful tradesman or professional man, having reached a certain stage in his career, would purchase land on the outskirts of his home town and commission a house tailored to his needs and tastes.

TOWN BUILDINGS
(*Illustrated Times* 1861)

26

JOHN BRIGHT'S HOME AT ONE ASH, ROCHDALE
(*Illustrated London News* 1889)

Often, part of his intention would be to impress his friends and business associates, so his house was liable to be a miniature version of the stately homes of the aristocrats he aspired to equal—turrets and towers, even belfries and battlements, might appear in the most improbable contexts. But where excess was avoided, such houses successfully achieved a scaled-down version of gracious living, well adapted to the new pattern of society.

Bedford Park, on the western outskirts of London, was one of the earliest attempts to *plan* a suburb, rather than simply let it happen. An enterprising landowner and the well-known architect Norman Shaw conceived, planned and created an estate comprising houses which for their day were attractive as well as functional, together with a club-house, inn and co-operative stores, all in a setting of trees and gardens. Designed for a middle-class community, it was a realistic and successful compromise between town and country living: *Harpers Magazine* in 1881 described it as 'the prettiest and pleasantest

BEDFORD PARK
(*Harper's Magazine* 1881)

27

MORNING PRAYER
(E. Prentis in *Family Devotion* c1845)

townlet in England . . . a Utopia in brick and paint'. But such ventures remained
the exception; most building was unplanned and undisciplined, meeting the needs of the
individual but flouting those of the community.

Within such homes as these, the way of life we think of as characteristically Victorian
was able to express itself. These were essentially family houses, designed to accommodate
father, mother and a quantity of children, together with such maiden aunts or widowed
cousins as had attached themselves to the nuclear family, plus the necessary servants
ranging in number from one to four or more according to means or requirements. The
way of life lived in these homes was essentially a family life, centred on the domestic
group, occasionally opening its doors to others for Christmas parties or birthdays, but
for the most part inward-looking and self-contained.

Just as, on their country estates, the aristocrats continued to maintain substantially
the same way of life as their forefathers, so their tenants, the farmers and farmworkers
who had resisted the pull to the towns, for the most part went on living in the traditional
ways, inhabiting the farms and cottages in which their fathers and grandfathers had lived.

To the sentimental Victorians, these rustic homes seemed idyllic survivals of an older,
simpler, more picturesque way of life, free from modern rush and care. But in reality
the inhabitants of the average rural cottage lived in hardly better conditions than their

SUSSEX COTTAGE INTERIOR
(*Century Magazine* 1885)

SURREY FARMHOUSE
(*English Illustrated Magazine* 1890)

LABOURER'S COTTAGE AT EAST MORDEN, DORSET
(*Illustrated London News* 1846)

former neighbours who had migrated to the town. True, country life was spacious compared with the overcrowded towns; but it was also liable to be damp, inconvenient and labour-making.

A few enlightened landowners recognised that their tenants deserved something better. Here and there, model homes and even model villages were built. But not everyone had the time, let alone the money and the inclination, to design attractive housing for the workers. Industry was in a hurry. To house their labour force, manufac-

MODEL COTTAGE BUILT BY LORD VERNON FOR HIS FARMWORKERS,
SUDBURY NEAR DERBY
(*Illustrated London News* 1869)

MINERS' COTTAGES AT LONG BENTON, NEAR NEWCASTLE
(Samuel Smiles *Lives of the Engineers: George & Robert Stephenson* 1857)

turers threw up houses as rapidly as possible, careless of any other consideration but those of speed and cost. In the neighbourhood of mines and mills, graceless little houses stretched in uncompromising rows across what had been fields and hills, as though to deny that the land beneath had any natural shape or contour. A hundred years later, a large proportion of the working people of Britain would still be living in these squalid, shabby, rural slums.

WILD COURT, SEVEN DIALS, LONDON
(Sketch in *Report of Common Lodging Houses* 1855)

At least the rural slums were surrounded by open space. In the towns, space was a luxury that few could afford. Here the working people lived in rooms in old houses, built one next to another, rented from landlords who generally—and understandably—lived elsewhere. The accommodation was of the crudest; such facilities as existed were communal. The pressure of a rapidly increasing urban population meant that homes were hard to come by, so landlords needed to do nothing to make them attractive.

There was every encouragement towards overcrowding, none towards improving the premises or doing anything except ensure that they did not actually fall down and thus lose their value as a source of income. One room in the building above housed seven people—one bed sleeping a man, three teenage daughters and their brother, the other their lodgers, a man and his wife. In another room, four families—eighteen persons in all—lived with one bed per family, with no partitions or privacy of any sort.

Within such homes, only rarely could the Victorian ideal of a happy domestic life be maintained. The *British Workman,* one of several publications produced by the middle classes to encourage the working classes, kept this ideal always before the worker's eyes; but only the most fortunate could hope to come near attaining it, however much they accepted the ideal itself as valid.

Insurmountable obstacles stood between the aspiring working man and his ideal. Long working hours kept the working members of the household out of the home—and this often included the wife and sometimes the children as well. In their leisure hours, the lack of comfort and facilities encouraged the children out into the streets for amusement, the husband and often the wife to the pubs for warmth and consolation. So home, for many, became little more than a pad for sleeping, a convenient place for laundry and other household tasks. Often, too, it was a workshop for home industries, whereby the wife and children tried to supplement the husband's earnings—the women chainmakers of Cradley, in the Black Country, would work half the week in the 'shop' for as little as 40 to 50 old pence; a chain which only a skilled worker could make in less than half an hour would earn her one old penny. Under such circumstances, the working class home could rarely fulfil its role as the natural focus of family life.

The scandal of the slums was too blatant to be ignored; they became a prime target for the philanthropists. Their first efforts took the form of simple charity, giving food and clothing to deserving cases, but enlightened people saw that a more radical solution was required. On the one hand, working conditions had to be changed—Shaftesbury's Factory Act of 1844 was just one of many legislatory acts which regulated the permissible degree of exploitation. On the other hand, housing conditions were improved. Later, municipal authorities were to take over the job of housing the under-privileged, but the start was made by benefactors like George Peabody and Baroness Burdett-Coutts, who financed projects to provide model dwellings for the industrious working classes. Many of these buildings still stand, seeming to us oppressive, claustrophobic, more like prisons than homes. It is only when we compare them with what they replaced that we can appreciate their merits. For all their faults, they provided the working class family with living conditions in which a decent, self-respecting family life was possible.

A ONE ROOM HOME
(Robert Barnes *Quiver* 1891)

32

Chapter Three

The Victorians At Work

IF there was one subject more than another which inspired the Victorians to pomposity, it was work. They were disposed to refer to it as 'honest toil', and to credit it with ennobling qualities conferring spiritual as well as material benefits. When Jerome K. Jerome in *Three Men in a Boat* wrote, 'I like work; it fascinates me. I can sit and look at it for hours,' his joke derived its force from the fact that his readers had been brought up to believe that work was something sacred. Everyone enters the world, the doctrine ran, with a certain portion of labour allotted to him; it is his sacred duty to carry out his task. 'Blessed is he who has found his work,' Carlyle wrote in *Past and Present*. 'Let him ask no other blessedness.' The attitude received its definitive visual statement in Ford Madox Brown's painting *Work*, while the writings of Samuel Smiles provided its gospel.

It goes without saying that Carlyle, Madox Brown and Smiles were all middle class; this religion of work was a middle-class creed. But the upper classes were shamed into at any rate a pretence of worship at the same altar. The men liked to have at least a nominal job—a comfortable sinecure at Court, say—to give them the illusion of participating in the national effort; while their womenfolk went in for charity and good works, some with genuine good intent, some with social motives, others simply to quiet their own consciences.

As for the lower classes, few of them would have considered work to be in any way sacred, despite the continual barrage of propaganda to that effect directed at them by the books and magazines and tracts and sermons prepared for them by the middle classes. But then it was the lower classes who had to do the dirty work.

And yet even among the common workers there must have been many who shared the sense of Britain's commercial eminence, and might have echoed the sentiments of that archetypal middle-class journalist, George Augustus Sala:

Coming home from abroad often, with an intelligent foreigner, when his agonies of sea-sickness have subsided and we are bearing swiftly on our way towards the Pool of London, I clap my companion on the back and cry, Look around, and see the glory

33

of England. Not in huge armies nor in granite forts shall be found our pride and our strength. Behold them, O intelligent person of foreign extraction! in yonder forest of masts, in the flags of every nation that fly from those tapering spars, in the great argosies of commerce that congregate from every port in the world . . . After this flourishing exordium I enter into some rapid details concerning the tonnage and import dues of the port of London.

('Twice Round the London Clock', 1858)

Men's work during the Victorian age was much like men's work in any other, only dirtier and more squalid. Compared with earlier periods, the difference was that so much more was now done communally, in mills and factories, as opposed to the home industries or small workshops which had formerly been the general rule. Compared with our own age, much less was done with machines, much more by hand.

Manufacturing tools for the world to use, hewing coal to drive the machines, keeping the flow of commerce in motion, building homes for the ever-growing population—all Britain was a restless sea of activity, continuously in ferment except for a few temporary calm patches such as when the American Civil War cut off cotton supplies to the Lancashire mills, bringing one of Britain's biggest industries to near standstill—and the country close to riot and revolution.

Working conditions and rates of pay were the result of bargaining, in which the employer held the stronger cards until the Trades Unions were legalised in 1871. Legislation, from the 1840s onwards, limited the worst abuses, but the glorious industrial development of the age had its continual dark underside of injustice and exploitation.

SCYTHE GRINDERS AT SHEFFIELD
(*Illustrated London News* 1865)

UNDERCUTTING A THIN COAL
(Margery May in the *English Illustrated Magazine* 1889)

There was a lot of work to be done—but fortunately for the employers there were a lot of people ready and anxious to do it. Employers could shop around for the cheapest labour they could get—which in many industries meant employing women, who did not expect to be paid so much, and gave less trouble into the bargain. (Among the Bradford wool-combers in the 1870s, a woman would accept 12 shillings a week where a man would demand 18 shillings for the same work.) In 1844, the textile mills of Yorkshire and Lancashire were employing more women than men, and half the 'men' were boys under 18. Women also worked beside men in the fields and down the mines.

WOMEN MINERS ON THE PIT BROW
(*Graphic* 1878)

DRESSMAKERS' WORKROOM
(*British Workman* 1868)

BOX-MAKING AT HOME IN THE EAST END OF LONDON
(*Cassell's Family Magazine* 1890s)

While it would be wrong to assume that all women workers were invariably ill-treated and exploited, there is no doubt that many were so. This was particularly true of industries where there were no men to fight for better conditions, such as the dressmaking trade, where long hours, low wages and appalling working conditions were normal. Another area of special abuse was the home industries, where families carried out work such as matchbox making, bead threading or nail making in their kitchen or living room, at pitifully small rates. (As late as 1903, matchbox makers were paid $2\frac{1}{4}$ old pence a *gross*—144—and had to buy their own paste and hemp!)

The most scandalous area of exploitation was in the employment of children. By the time Victoria came to the throne the evils had already been recognised and the most notorious abuses checked. It was no longer possible to send children of 6 or 7 to work for 16 hours a day underground, or to turn them loose into the fields or streets to fend for themselves when there was no work for them. But though factories were now subject to inspection, and hours for children under 13 were limited, the Mines Report of 1842 showed that appalling exploitation was still normal. Lord Shaftesbury's 1844 Factory Act took a major step towards greater control against fierce opposition from economists who believed that employers and workers should be left free to make their own agreements, unfettered by outside interference; but by now the tragic consequences of

CHILDREN WORKING IN BRICKYARDS
(*Graphic* 1871)

37

LETTING CHILDREN DOWN
A COAL MINE
(*Westminster Review* c1842)

laissez-faire were too obvious to be ignored. From the 1840s on, working hours were gradually reduced, working standards gradually raised. It was not until the 1870s, though, that the normal working conditions of the people of England can be said to have reached even a tolerable level.

It is noteworthy that all the earlier reforms were initiated and carried through by the middle and upper classes, not by the efforts of the working people themselves. Centuries of subjection could not be eradicated in a single generation; it was only when the middle classes had awakened the working people to their essential human rights that the great mass of the population began to feel they had any claim to determine their own fortunes, and to expect a say in the way their country was run.

OFFICE CLERKS
(*Judy* 1890)

"The girl raised her eyes,
started, and turned white."

A LADY TYPIST
(*Windsor* 1901)

THE UNDERWRITING ROOM AT LLOYDS
(*Graphic* 1886)

The white-collar worker stood in less need of protective legislation. The aristocracy might affect to look down on a family whose breadwinner was 'in trade', but this bothered only a minority; as a rule, a banker or a broker or a member of Lloyds knew it was his class who truly kept the country going and growing, and unless he cherished unnatural social ambitions, he could feel pretty content with his lot. Even his clerks, though their work may seem to us—and doubtless seemed to them—intolerably laborious, were not as a rule ill-paid or unduly exploited.

When women started to invade the office, from about 1870, they suffered little of the exploitation that working class women underwent in factory or workshop. The Prudential Assurance Company, who employed some 170 'daughters of professional men' in 1881,

AMATEUR NAVVIES AT OXFORD: UNDERGRADUATES MAKING A ROAD
AS SUGGESTED BY MR RUSKIN
(*Graphic* 1874)

provided its young ladies with a restaurant offering an 8d lunch, a library of new books, a piano, a choral society, opportunity for exercise on a flat roof ('skipping is the favourite amusement') and a separate staircase from that used by the male clerks ('any attempt at flirtation is sternly discouraged').

But 'real' work was work which was achieved by the sweat of one's brow. John Ruskin knew the difference. 'Which of us,' he asked in *Sesame and Lilies*, 'is to do the hard and dirty work—and for what pay? Who is to do the pleasant and clean work, and for what pay?' And so, as Slade Professor of Fine Art at Oxford, he sent his students to rebuild a patch of bad road at Hinksey. They came—some of them by cab—and they built the road: and if they did not do it as well as the professionals, at least they learnt something about the difference between clean and pleasant work and hard and dirty work, and would be less likely, when they went out into the world, to prate about the sanctity of work and the dignity of honest labour.

Chapter Four

Supplies And Services

ONE part of the basic thinking behind the Industrial Revolution was that, if workers were organised so that each man did one job well rather than many jobs less well, manpower would be used more efficiently, productivity would increase and costs would fall.

What applied to work applied also to other spheres of life, notably to the provision of supplies and services. The trend throughout the Victorian age was for the citizen to become a specialist, master of one trade rather than jack of many, expecting his fellows to complement his contribution by providing other services in return. Socially, he looked to the community to do more and more for him. At the beginning of the period he expected Authority to protect him against foes and criminals, and to safeguard his basic rights, but little more. As the age proceeded, he came to expect to be able to call on an increasing diversity of public services to carry out tasks which had previously been left to private initiative; and he accepted the fact that he would have to pay for them by increased rates and taxes, and by giving up a certain degree of freedom of action. He trusted that by handing over his freedom to democratically elected institutions, such as Town Councils, his surrender would not be exploited.

So long as society was primarily rural, it was normal practice for people to supply most of their own everyday needs. They wove their own cloth and made their own dress, they grew their own fruit and vegetables and reared their own meat, they baked their own bread and brewed their own beer, they built their own homes and made their own furnishings. Only for extraordinary needs—when they required goods like cooking utensils or tools not easily fabricated at home, or when they craved imported luxuries like spices and silks—did they have to call on specialist services, either visiting the artisan direct or going to markets where his wares were for sale.

In town environments this pattern changed, and the practice grew of one man, say, baking for his neighbours, depending on them in return for his groceries and vegetables. This is the background against which the provision of supplies in Victorian Britain must be seen; for the pattern is a steady swing towards interdependence throughout the

41

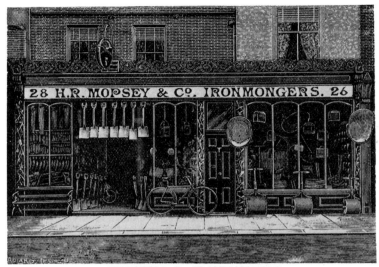

MOPSEY & Co, IRONMONGERS
(*Illustrated London* 1893)

LEWIS'S DEPARTMENT STORE, LIVERPOOL
(*Illustrated London News* 1883)

(Left) VILLAGE STORE
(*Sunday at Home* 1867)

(Above) PETER ROBINSON'S
OXFORD STREET
(*Illustrated London News* 1891)

STREET TRADERS: MUFFINS
(*Dawn of Day* 1887)

STREET TRADERS: MEAT
(*Dawn of Day* 1888)

43

DINING ROOMS IN BUCKLERSBURY
(William M'Connell, Sala's *Twice round the London Clock* 1858)

entire period. At first, shops were generally on a small and local scale, family businesses for the most part: gradually, in the more populous districts, they evolved into larger establishments, employing large staffs and meeting many needs under a single roof.

Shops have one serious drawback: the housewife has to leave home to visit them. So in all ages, private traders have found they could filch some business from the shops by bringing goods to the customer's door. To meet such competition, the shops had to provide their own delivery services. In Victorian times, wherever business warranted such efforts, housekeepers found they could do most of their everyday shopping without leaving the home. In an establishment of any standing, the cook would expect her regular tradesmen—dairyman, butcher, baker, grocer, greengrocer—to call on her every morning for orders which would often be delivered an hour or two later. In poorer areas, street traders would tour the alleys and courts, crying their wares to attract their customers.

Drinking away from home had long been a regular feature of British social life, but until Victorian times few ate abroad except travellers and bachelors. Now a third class was added: the businessmen, who often lived on the outskirts of towns, too far from their place of work to go home for their mid-day meal. So dining rooms made their appearance in commercial centres, and increased in number and choice to match their growing clientele.

BARMAIDS IN A VICTORIAN PUBLIC HOUSE
(1870s)

LAMPLIGHTER
(*British Workman* 1863)

LONDON NIGHTMEN
(Mayhew's *London Labour and the London Poor*
1862)

Growing leisure and increasing opportunity for recreation created a demand for other types of refreshment facilities. Victorian towns, London in particular, saw all kinds of establishment spring up—supper rooms, cigar divans, cafés, music halls, as well as the traditional public house which was generally grander and smarter than the old gin palaces. At many of these establishments there was entertainment as well as refreshment.

The Victorian city was a vast co-operative enterprise. Each citizen depended on his

45

fellows at every turn. He relied on other people to look after his money for him, to deliver his letters, to send a fire engine if his house caught fire, to remove refuse from his house, to light his streets and to keep them in good repair.

FIRE ENGINE OF THE METROPOLITAN FIRE BRIGADE
(*Illustrated London News* 1889)

In the country, a man was more his own master, but his freedom was bought at a price—life was neither so comfortable nor so convenient. Village streets were unmade-up and unlit; and though the village shop might double as the post office, you could not expect it to provide the same standard of service. Townsmen were apt to be disconcerted. Sydney Smith reported on a country visit, 'It is a place with only one post a day . . . in the country I always fear that creation will expire before tea-time.'

EVENING IN ESSEX
(*English Illustrated Magazine* 1889)

Chapter Five

Education

Yes, he had heer'd of God, who made the world. Couldn't exactly recollec' when he'd heer'd on him, but he had, most sartenly. Didn't know when the world was made, or how anybody could do it. It must have taken a long time. It was afore his time, 'or yourn either, sir' . . . Had never heer'd of France, but had heer'd of Frenchmen . . . The stars was fire, or they wouldn't shine. They didn't make it warm, they was too small. Didn't know any use they was of. Didn't know how far they was off: a jolly lot higher than the gas lights some of them was . . .
(14-year-old coster's boy, questioned by Henry Mayhew in 1851)

DURING the first half of Victoria's reign it was possible for a child to reach adulthood without having received any formal education whatever. Schools existed, and in bewildering variety: there were dame's schools and village schools, parish and private schools, Ragged and National schools, grammar and public schools. But there was no obligation for children to attend any of them. Well-to-do or ambitious parents naturally wanted to see their children educated, but at the bottom end of the social scale this meant not only paying for the schooling but also forfeiting the child's earnings. For a family close to the poverty line, this was too great a price to pay.

The earnest Victorians believed that spiritual welfare was largely dependent on intellectual enlightenment ('Let knowledge grow from more to more,' wrote Tennyson, their leading poetical spokesman, but added, 'but more of reverence in us dwell'), and the intellectual and therefore spiritual darkness in which so many of their fellow-countrymen walked was consequently intolerable. 'The community suffers a huge amount of mischief in every way from the idleness and ignorance, too readily seduced to positive crime, among the poor neglected youth of our towns,' wrote the *Illustrated London News* in 1857.

And so it came about that during the second half of the reign, the educational scene was completely transformed. Though there were differences of opinion about methods, nobody seriously questioned the desirability of giving every child a chance to be educated.

47

RAGGED SCHOOL
(*Graphic* 1871)

DAME'S SCHOOL
(A. Rankley, reproduced in *Illustrated London News* 1856)

There had already been periodic attempts to create a national educational system. At last, in 1870, Forster's epoch-making Education Act provided the framework for such a system. Elementary education was made available to all, at a price within the means of all. Ten years later education became compulsory for children up to 10; twenty years later popular education was made free.

Children like Mayhew's street boy, quoted above, if they received any education at all, received it in its most primitive form. Before 1870, the 'Ragged' schools were often the only schooling available to the children of the penniless poor. The first Ragged School was founded before Victoria came to the throne, by John Pounds in Portsmouth; other philanthropists followed his example, and by 1855 there were 150 of them. They depended entirely upon charity, as indeed did most schools at this date. The education provided was of the simplest—one doubts if the girl in this illustration is likely to learn much from her fellow-student, only a little older than herself. But simply to be in such an environment was better then hanging about the home or playing in the street.

The National schools, run by the Church of England, were often managed by courageous volunteers under the most discouraging circumstances. One such school, at Plaistow, was housed in a shed leaning against the wall of a grocer's shop. The only light came from the roof, into which two sashes from a greenhouse had been inserted. 'The glass is happily much broken, which, together with the rents in the boards, provides for ventilation. In cold weather this is quite sufficient for most people's feelings . . .'

Country children were often better off than their counterparts in town. The good 'dame' of the Dame's school, often held in her own kitchen, was not likely to be qualified to do more than instruct her neighbour's children in the basic rudiments of learning, but at least the small numbers ensured individual attention.

Many villages and most small towns had a parish or some other type of charity school, maintained by a local big family or some other person or body, or simply by a group of local citizens. If the school were well endowed, there might be a qualified teacher or two; if not, the job would more likely fall to the vicar's wife or an unmarried daughter. Either way, such a school, catering for mixed classes of widely differing ages and abilities, cannot have provided more than the most meagre sip from the fountains of knowledge.

For those who could afford it, the first stages in education were taken at home with a governess. This was one of the few respectable jobs open to middle-class girls, particularly the daughters of the impecunious but prolific clergy: supply greatly exceeded the demand, though most can have had but little qualification, let alone vocation, for the job. The status of the governess, like her wages, was low: she was neither a member of the family nor a servant, and was generally despised by both—and often by her pupils into the bargain. In the country she would be residential, in town she would more likely be a 'daily'. Either way, for an average annual income of about £40, she was expected to instruct her charges in—to quote a typical advertisement of the 1850s— 'the usual branches of a solid English education'.

Above a certain age—7 or 8 in most cases—the boys would generally be taught by a tutor, often a local clergyman supplementing his inadequate stipend. Alternatively,

GOVERNESS AND PUPILS
(E. F. Brewtnall *Sunday Magazine* 1873)

HANOVER STREET BOARD SCHOOL
(*Graphic* 1877)

they would be sent to one of a growing number of private academies designed to prepare them for their public schools—hence their name of 'preparatory' schools.

Holmes: 'Look at those big, isolated clumps of buildings rising up above the slates, like brick islands in a lead-coloured sea.'
Watson: 'The Board Schools.'
Holmes: 'Lighthouses, my boy! Beacons of the future! Capsules with hundreds of bright little seeds in each, out of which will spring the wiser, better England of the future.'
(Conan Doyle, 'Memoirs of Sherlock Holmes'—The Naval Treaty)

Holmes was enthusing about the schools built by the London School Board, which—along with other such boards throughout the country—came into being as a result of Forster's 1870 Education Act. This enacted that there must be elementary education available for all, which faced the responsible local authorities with a sizable problem. The newly formed London School Board in 1871 found it had 574,693 pupils to cater for, and only 261,158 places in schools which could be classed as efficient. So a crash building programme was initiated to supplement the existing voluntary schools.

The 1870 Act gave discretionary powers to local boards to enforce attendance at school on children who were not otherwise learning or working. In 1880 attendance became compulsory for children between 5 and 10: in 1893 the upper age was raised to 11, in 1899 to 12. There was considerable resentment against this compulsion. The

A LONDON SCHOOL BOARD CAPTURE UNDER THE ARCHES OF
CHARING CROSS STATION
(Illustrated London News 1871)

education was cheap—9d a week was the maximum, and even this could be remitted in case of hardship—but even so, many parents objected to paying for something they did not want. Many tried to avoid sending their children to school, and would either hide them at the approach of the inspector, or lie about their age.

Things were very different for the sons of the wealthy. The great public schools were not perfect, but they offered a far better education than anything the less well-off could obtain. Their insistence on the traditional disciplines—the classics and formal mathematics—was hardly conducive to a well-rounded education; nevertheless they contrived to create a fairly civilised type of human being. Socially their influence was less admirable. Thomas Arnold at Rugby, and other reformers elsewhere, fought to create an educational environment which would produce gentlemen rather than the barbarians the younger Arnold was to deride. But the public schools continued to live by traditions which became less and less relevant to the way the country as a whole was moving.

Hardly less hidebound than the public schools were the Grammar schools, many of them founded in Tudor times by enlightened patrons, and maintained since then by private endowments. They provided the middle classes with an opportunity for secondary education; their inferiors had virtually no such opportunity at all.

The education of girls lagged behind that of boys. There were a few endowed schools for girls—the foundation of the Girls' Public Day School Trust in 1872 was a rare instance of enlightened thinking—but the general feeling was that girls could benefit from education less than boys, and the opportunities available to them were greatly limited.

THE SIXTH FORM AT MARLBOROUGH COLLEGE
(*Graphic* 1886)

THE ALL-ROUND MAN, OXFORD
(*Graphic*, 1882)

NEWNHAM GIRL IN HER STUDY
(*Graphic* 1887)

The university was the logical next step for the public school boy, unless he was destined for the army or navy. It offered a continuation of much the same sort of life as he had known at school. Despite reforms designed to impose more enlightened standards, the universities maintained a traditional way of life hardly at all in keeping with the requirements of modern education. The growing number of scholarship students, to whom educational success was an important factor in career making, resulted in a healthy infiltration from the middle and even occasionally from the working classes. But the universities remained very largely privileged playgrounds for the sons of the rich.

The introduction of university education for women was bitterly contested on 'woman's-place-is-the-home' grounds, which remind us that the Victorians were quite capable of allowing the inconsistencies and bigotries of their social attitudes to warp their intellectual judgments. However, common sense was permitted a limited triumph in this case: colleges for women were established at Oxford and Cambridge, though it was a century before women students achieved equal status with men.

Education for a purpose was a concept which chimed in perfectly with Victorian middle-class thinking. Unfortunately it conflicted with the upper-class devotion to classical learning as the only true touchstone of education. Organisations such as City Companies managed ultimately to introduce a few function-oriented establishments into the system, but it was only after bitter fighting against the educational establishment.

With art it was a different matter. Art was something the Victorians respected and valued, and in its creation they were ready to agree that special disciplines—or rather lack of disciplines—were appropriate. Just as they accepted that the artist cannot be

ROYAL ACADEMY SCHOOL
(*Magazine of Art* 1888)

treated like another man, so art students need not be expected to behave like other students.

Many Victorians saw that it was unfair to deny to the parents the new opportunities which were being made available to their children. Though efforts to help the adult working classes to educate themselves were sporadic, and dependent on individual effort and charity, a wide variety of working men's institutes, colleges and reading rooms were founded from 1854 onwards. At the Bloomsbury Working Men's College, budding working class artists were privileged to be taught by none other than Ruskin himself!

Most of the great museums of Britain were founded in Victorian times. By the end of the century almost every major city had its own municipal museum and art gallery, generally owing its inception and maintenance to local benefactors. It was recognised that they provided instruction as well as recreation to the working man; unfortunately there was a large body of opinion which held that they should not be made available to him on the one day he was free to visit them—for on Sunday he should be performing his religious duties. It is significant that, whether deliberately or not, the case for opening museums on Sunday was based not on intellectual improvement but moral welfare. 'The great argument in favour of opening museums and picture galleries on Sundays is that they would be an alternative to the public houses, which are so seductive for the working man on cold, wet and gloomy Sunday afternoons.' (*Graphic 1879*.) Even so, it was not until 1896 that the working man was allowed to visit the London museums on the Sabbath Day.

EVENING CLASSES FOR WORKING MEN AT LOUTH
(*British Workman* 1862)

Chapter Six

Travel And Communication

MANY of the changes which took place during the Victorian period were complex and difficult to evaluate—shifts in social attitudes or moral standards are hard to measure and lend themselves to a wide range of interpretation. But the material changes which accompanied these intangible shifts are more easily assessed; and most easily, the extraordinary speed-up of all kinds of communication. At the beginning of the period, we find Tom Brown's coach journey to Rugby described as an event of capital importance: at the end, Sherlock Holmes and the faithful Watson leap into West Country expresses with hardly more deliberation than hailing a hansom. And if man had found how to travel fast, he had found how to send his messages even faster—thanks to telephone and telegraph, he could send instructions or receive news in a matter of minutes almost anywhere in the world.

As an end in themselves, rapid communications are nothing. The Victorians themselves recognised that a man is no better off for being able to travel at 50 mph, if he merely travels from an empty fruitless life in one place to an empty fruitless life in another. But rapid travel provides a striking example of the power of material factors to open the way for social and moral changes. The effects of the new mobility were incalculable. It broke down insular attitudes—people could get about and see how their fellow-countrymen lived: the attendance at the Great Exhibition could not have been so great if it had not been for low-cost rail transport. It also meant that shared but scattered interests could make contact more easily—societies could foregather, merchants and businessmen could shop around, trades unionists could keep in touch with their fellows, all as never before.

When Victoria came to the throne, the primary form of communication throughout Britain was the stage-coach service. A complex network of routes spanned the country, with relay horses ready and waiting at strategic points—Hounslow, a typical posting town, maintained 2,500 horses: an important posting inn might have 500 horses of its own. Warned by a distant horn from the approaching coach, the ostlers would get fresh horses ready to switch with the same precise urgency as wheels on a modern racing car.

At the height of the coaching era, in the 1830s, there were 60 mail-coaches and many hundreds of stage-coaches regularly plying the roads of Britain, as well as thousands of private vehicles. The coaches were highly sophisticated vehicles, superbly functional in design, capable of taking full advantage of the new macadamised roads. By using the fastest coach—the Mail—a traveller could cover the 200-odd miles between London and Liverpool in 23 hours, an average of nearly 9 mph. But this was achieved at the cost of great physical discomfort, even inside the coach; there were only the briefest of halts for refreshment while horses were being changed, and the price was high—6d a mile (equivalent to well over 10p today). Consequently coach travel was only for the fortunate few or for special occasions. The majority of people, if they had to travel, went on foot, or by the slower carrier's waggon; more generally, though, they stayed where they were.

It is arguable that the railways brought about a greater social revolution than any other factor in British history. Opposed by different sections of the public on differing grounds—doctors thought the high speeds would prove fatal, economists reckoned the railways could not hope to show a profit, farmers feared they would frighten livestock— the benefits were nevertheless so patent that their triumph was assured. The first passenger-carrying service was opened between Stockton and Darlington in 1825, and Liverpool and Manchester were linked five years later. Throughout the 1830s progress was slow but steady; by 1838 there were 500 miles of track. Then in the 1840s things accelerated rapidly. By 1843, 2,400 miles had been laid. In 1848 there were 5,000 and it was calculated that close on 200,000 'navigators' were at work, constructing a network of routes which flew over valleys, burrowed beneath hills, pierced or skirted towns, linking every part of the country to every other. Writing in 1837, a Mr McCulloch, while foreseeing that 'rail-roads will most likely be established at no distant period

'IT'S THE *COMET*, AND YOU MUST BE QUICK AS LIGHTNING'
(Alken *The Road* 1837)

SLUM CHILDREN ON A RAIL EXCURSION TO THE COUNTRY
(*Scribner's Magazine* 1892)

between all the great towns of the empire where the ground is at all practicable,' could add, 'The advantages likely to be derived from the extension of the system to other parts of the country have, we believe, been a good deal exaggerated.' Sixty years later, another statistician, J Holt Schooling, reckoned that British railways matched the circumference of the world every 40 minutes of the day or night.

Early rail travel was exceedingly uncomfortable, particularly for third-class passengers, who had to stand in open trucks and put up with whatever the weather was doing. Even this did not prevent it becoming popular—in its first year, 1830, the Liverpool & Manchester Railway was carrying an average of over 1,200 passengers a day, and the 1841 census had to take into account 4,003 men and 893 females travelling by rail or canal on the night of 6 June. The companies were indignant when, in 1844, they were required by law to run at least one 'parliamentary' train each day on their tracks, providing covered third-class accommodation at a penny a mile, but to their delight they found that cheap transport was at least as profitable as any other. Now that people were offered the possibility of travelling easily about the country, nothing could stop them. So it was that, virtually within the space of a decade, Britain was transformed from a collection of more or less isolated regions, scantily linked by a slow and costly service, to a single national entity, served by a comprehensive and integrated system enabling anyone to travel at a modest price from anywhere to anywhere else in a matter of hours.

The coming of the railways meant that, for the first time, the great mass of the English people could see for themselves what other parts of their country were like. Country people could venture into the towns and cities; town people could see the hills and the sea.

It was not only passengers who benefited from rail travel. In 1838 Parliament permitted mails to go by rail, and by 1841 most mails were in fact so carried. Industry and commerce, which had provided the impetus for the development of railways in the first place, now took full advantage of their services for the rapid transport of goods and materials.

The railways offered a solution for a problem which was already critical more than a century ago—the overcrowding of London's streets. Today we take underground railways for granted: it is hard to realise what a revolutionary concept they were, and what vision and courage it required to make them a reality. The first line in London—the Metropolitan between Paddington and Holborn—was opened in January 1863. By 1865 it was carrying some 20,000 passengers a day. Unfortunately, the population and business were growing so fast that London continued to be overcrowded!

But the railways could not go everywhere. They had emptied the great trunk roads of Britain of traffic, leaving them virtually deserted until the coming of the motor-car.

CROWDED LONDON STREET
(*Graphic* 1875)

59

HORSE BUS: 'THE AMENITIES OF A WET DAY'
(*Leisure Hour* 1870)

(Right) LONDON HANSOM CAB
(*Leisure Hour* 1892)

(Below) CARRIER'S WAGGON
(*British Workman* 1861)

CANAL LIFE: ON THE ROAD
(*Illustrated London News* 1874)

But local goods traffic was still handled by the carrier's waggon, local passenger traffic by the horse bus and the cab.

Trains and buses allowed the less well-to-do sections of society to share the mobility enjoyed by their carriage-owning betters. Similarly it was the cycle which gave them the individual freedom that the horse gave its owner. Bicycles and tricycles were the subject of intense development in the 1850s and 1860s—the *Mechanic's Magazine* for the period seems to contain little else but cycle projects. In the 1870s a dazzling variety of more or less successful models were made available to the public. At first the price was high—a good class of machine around 1880 cost £20 or more, even a cheap model cost £12 (equivalent to over four times this sum today); so at first cycling was a leisure pursuit for the middle and upper classes. But the great vogue for cycling brought prices tumbling, and in the early 1890s, half a million cycles were being built every year. They put personal transport within the reach of all, allowing townsfolk like H G Wells's office-clerk and shop-assistant heroes to get about and see places as never before.

The great expansion of the British canal system had taken place in the earlier phase of the Industrial Revolution—the only solution which at that time offered itself for the large-scale transport of bulky goods and materials. A comprehensive network had been completed by about 1830—and then came the railways. At first it looked as though they would drive the barges from the canals as they had driven the coaches from the roads, but after an initial setback, the canal business recovered its former prosperity and more. Manufacturers learned that speed is not everything; the barge made up in sheer capacity what it lacked in speed, offering a positive economic advantage. So the canals, which together with the navigable rivers formed an integrated system of more than 5,000 miles of inland waterway, continued to play a vital role in the nation's transport until well into the twentieth century.

61

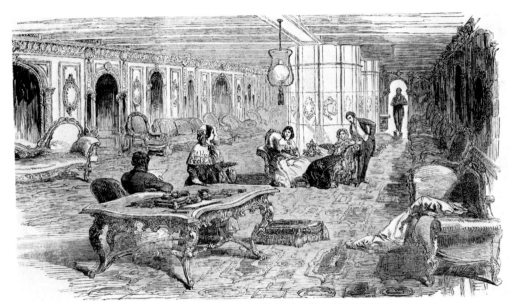

THE GRAND SALOON OF THE *ATLANTIC*
(*Illustrated London News* 1850)

STEERAGE PASSENGERS CROSSING THE ATLANTIC, ABOUT 1850
(Cassell's *History of England*)

USING THE TELEPHONE
(*Graphic* 1883)

The steamship was securely established when the Victorian age began, but it was far from replacing the sailing ship: steam and sail were to work side by side for several decades more. However, the ultimate triumph of steam was inevitable wherever speed and punctuality were important factors, and this applied particularly to pace-setting passenger routes such as the Atlantic crossing. Here, voyage times dropped from a typical 23 days eastward and 40 westward by sail, to 15 either way by steam in 1838 (*Great Western*), 8 in 1867 (*City of Paris*) and 5 in 1889 (*Philadelphia*).

Once speed had been achieved, consideration could be given to comfort. Iron and later steel hulls took the place of wood, enabling larger ships to be built: this meant that they could not only carry more passengers, but carry them more spaciously. At the beginning of the Victorian age, everyone who journeyed abroad, rich or poor, did so in confined discomfort: at the end of the age the well-to-do, at any rate, could sail in palatial luxury, and even the emigrant in the steerage could travel in relative comfort.

Now, at last, sea travel could be a pleasure in itself, not just an unavoidable ordeal to be suffered. Just as the railways provided not only a rapid practical means of land travel but also the opportunity for sightseeing and holidays, so the new steamships opened the way to pleasure voyages ranging from excursions among the Scottish Isles to round-the-world luxury cruises.

If it had become important to man to transport himself more rapidly and efficiently, it was hardly less important to improve the way he communicated with his fellows at a distance. The discovery by Wheatstone of a practical method of electric telegraphy, in the year before Victoria's accession, opened the way to a breakthrough in telecommunication. Two years later, an electric telegraph line was erected on the Great Western

63

Railway, and soon plans were being laid for the first submarine cable. In fact it was not until 1851 that the Channel cable was successfully laid; but thereafter there was a wave of cable-laying all over the world, culminating in the dramatic laying of the Atlantic cable by the *Great Eastern* in 1865. By 1862 there were 150,000 miles of telegraph in the world, 15,000 of them in Britain. They meant that news and information could be sent from almost any part of the world to any other in a matter of minutes, where before it might have taken weeks. The effect on business and administration was of course immeasurable.

On a more local scale, the invention of the telephone effected a similar revolution. After much research it was finally made available in 1878, and in the following year the Temple and the Law Courts were telephonically linked. As with the telegraph, the world was quick to exploit the new technology, and by 1890 the telephone was well-nigh universally adopted. The telephone completed what the railways had begun: they gave the final blow to the old isolation of man from man, community from community.

The most tantalizing of the elements—the air—continued to challenge. Flights by balloon were fairly common occurrences, a standard attraction at outdoor festivities; and they had even been put to a certain amount of practical use in scientific research and military communication. But as a means of regular transport, the flying machine was still not viable, nor would be until a genuinely dirigible craft could be developed. Experimentation continued throughout the age, but the air was not to be conquered during Victoria's lifetime.

BALLOONS AT CREMORNE GARDENS
(*Illustrated London News* 1859)

Chapter Seven

Recreation

HE Victorians were particularly good at entertainment. They were good at entertaining others—there was no lack of packaged amusement, supplied by professional purveyors. And they were good at entertaining themselves—do-it-yourself family entertainment had not yet been supplanted by the neighbourhood cinema and the television set. So they enjoyed a best-of-both-worlds diversity: their recreation took so many forms that we can show only a selection of them here.

They enjoyed themselves with a special gusto, perhaps because their leisure had to work so hard to make up for the general drabness of their working lives. We can laugh at the heavy-handed naivety of their melodrama or despise the extravagantly naturalistic staging of their plays: we can suspect that the standard of performance when the family gathered round the piano or staged its amateur theatricals was not specially brilliant: but we cannot withhold our admiration for the enthusiasm, imagination and initiative which the Victorians brought to the business of entertainment.

ENTERTAINMENT AT HOME

Victorian parties at home were not just drinks and chat, but more or less elaborately organised entertainments, mounted by hosts and guests for their own amusement. Everybody would be expected to take part in games like Charades. Most people, too, would be able to play the piano or sing; the piano was standard equipment in every well-furnished middle-class home, and kept for use as well as show. Dancing was not simply an excuse to hug girls to whom you were not yet engaged: it was a genuine and living tradition, and most regions of the country still retained their local styles with which most people would be familiar, and in which they would join spontaneously and unselfconsciously, just as the street children would respond instantly to a passing barrel-organ.

For solitary entertainment there was the novel, whose growth throughout the 19th century was a remarkable phenomenon, culminating in the mighty 'three-decker', 3-volume chronicles of mingled fortune and disaster which would be carried home

DANCING AT HOME—'TEN SHILLINGS A NIGHT'
(*London Society* 1865)

WELSH COLLIERS 'STEPPING'
(*Graphic* 1873)

CHARADES
(*London Society* 1864)

excitedly from a circulating library like Mudie's; hundreds and occasionally thousands of copies of a new book would be bought by Mudie's to satisfy its customers. From around 1850, usually as a result of some private benefaction, free public libraries began to spring up in the towns.

STAGE AND SPECTACLE

Stage entertainment took a great variety of forms. Legitimate theatre ranged from Shakespeare to sentimental melodrama. Boucicault's *The Colleen Bawn* was a special favourite in the latter category, frequently revived by popular request. Production styles tended towards the spectacular, as did those of pantomime; but while dramatic producers aimed at naturalistic representations of shipwrecks and horse-races, storms or the battle of Agincourt, pantomime spectacle reached its grand finale with magic transformation scenes which left reality as far behind as possible. Music halls provided the same mixture of realism and escape—tenderly sentimental ballads alternating with down-to-earth bawdy, a traditional English blend which once again belies our image of a puritan, uptight age. On the fringe of stage entertainment were such one-man shows as Woodin's entertainments, sensationally popular in the 1850s: he appeared alone on the stage in some 50 different characters in the course of the evening, successfully occupying 'that neutral ground which lies beyond the province of the drawing-room and stops short on the verge of the department of the stage.' Magic lanterns were a formative

BOUCICAULT'S *THE COLLEEN BAWN*—THE CAVE SCENE
(*Illustrated London News* 1860)

67

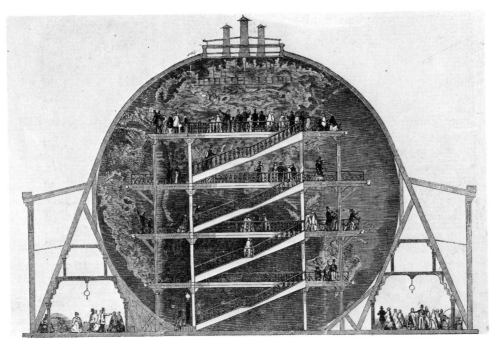

WYLD'S MODEL OF THE EARTH, LEICESTER SQUARE
(*Illustrated London News* 1851)

MAGIC LANTERN ENTERTAINMENT TO POOR CHILDREN
(*Graphic* 1889)

influence on many young imaginations besides those of Charles Dickens or Marcel Proust, and had great capacity for instruction as well as amusement. The same was true of Wyld's great walk-round model of the earth, a prominent feature of Leicester Square in the 1850s. For the music lover there were plenty of concerts and operas: the star system, though never so passionately maintained in Britain as in Vienna or Milan, none the less gave rise to fanaticism comparable with that displayed today for pop singers. Finally, there were the sacred oratorios—one of the few musical forms in which Victorian composers produced really worthwhile music, and which had the additional merit of gratifying both the artistic and the devout sections of society.

SPECTATOR SPORTS

Sport took different forms at different levels of society. This was an age in which spectator sports grew from minority pursuits to big business: the same popular fervour which had previously been limited to boxing and racing now spread to cricket and football, while more intimate games like golf and tennis became public spectacles as well as private pastimes. Walking matches were popular events—one of the few Victorian sports which has not retained its popularity. The most important sporting occasions were ones where for the great majority there was no question of participation: the Derby and the University boat race. These annual events were the excuse for great holiday excursions, wherein a happening which in one case lasted only a matter of seconds, the other twenty minutes or so, provided the occasion for a red-letter day in the annual calendar.

SIX-DAY WALKING MATCH AT THE AGRICULTURAL HALL
(*Graphic* 1878)

69

BOXING AT THE NATIONAL SPORTING CLUB
(Phil May 1897)

SHOOTING: 'A GOOD DAY'S WORK IN THE COVERS'
(*Graphic* 1882)

FISHING
(Cassell's *Family Magazine* 1889)

CROQUET
(*London Society* 1860s)

ARISTOCRATIC AMUSEMENTS

For the well-to-do, sport took the traditional form of killing animals in various ways. Even the busiest statesman could spare time from diplomacy or legislation to chase birds over a grouse moor or ride over the fields in pursuit of a fox. Sometimes he required the help of the lower classes: he employed gamekeepers all year round to ensure that his quarry would be there to be killed at the right place and the right time, and small boys would work from four in the morning till seven at night on the Yorkshire moors, beating up game for their betters. For the ladies and the curate, there would be a game of croquet on the lawn—a seemingly gentle affair which in fact offered quite as much outlet for the passions as any form of hunting.

COUNTRY FAIR
(*Scribner's Magazine* 1880)

71

ROSHERVILLE GARDENS
(*Windsor* 1897)

POPULAR PASTIMES

Those who could not afford to own or even rent a grouse moor or a stretch of trout stream had to take their fun as they found it. There was plenty to choose from, particularly in the towns. In the country, the annual fairs and travelling circuses were likely to be the only amusement apart from market days: townsfolk had not only their museums and galleries, but also zoos and popular out-of-town rendezvous like Rosherville Gardens, near Gravesend. Those who could make it to the seaside found all kinds of beach entertainment awaiting them: or one could head for the nearest woods or riverbank and enjoy a family picnic, with convenient cover for strolling couples. And even stay-at-homes had the parks, in which to be as active or as indolent as they wished.

Chapter Eight

Health And Sickness

ODAY most of us can expect to live to see our 70th birthdays: at the beginning of Victoria's reign we would have been lucky to see our 42nd. Similarly, the chances of a child surviving to adulthood were only half what they are today.

It was against this sombre background that the Victorians lived their lives and enacted the scenes illustrated in this book. Death was always waiting in the wings: it was not simply an ultimate inevitability, it was a daily possibility, and so they schooled themselves to face it with philosophic fatalism. At the same time, with that strange bravado which characterises the human being when faced with inescapable defeat, they chose to celebrate death in an elaborate ritual which concealed the face of tragedy behind a ceremonial mask. This explains why the British public, though sympathetic with their Queen's grief when Albert died, blamed her for allowing herself to decline into a recluse—'the Widow of Windsor'. The ritual acts of pious memory— the Albert Hall and Memorial, the Mausoleum at Frogmore and the trees and statues planted up and down the land—these were fine and fitting; but that she should give up attending to the affairs of her country was as blameworthy as that a Victorian housewife should cease running her home under the same circumstances.

This fatalistic attitude did not of course mean that the Victorians made no attempt to combat the forces of death. On the contrary; medical science made remarkable progress—anaesthetics were discovered, hospital conditions revolutionised, the importance of sanitation recognised, the nursing profession dignified, vaccination generally accepted, countless diseases and ailments identified and treatments evolved. Nevertheless, after sixty years of such progress, the expectation of life had been pushed up by a mere 5 years to 46, and 146 out of every 1,000 babies failed to survive their first year on earth.

Perhaps it was inevitable that one of the less fortunate aspects of this heightened status of medicine should have been the ossification of the medical establishment into a conversative, bigoted body which—for all its achievements—became something of a stumbling block to further progress. But the institutionalisation of medicine was on

FAMILY DOCTOR AT BEDSIDE
(c1870)

DEATH OF THE FIRST-BORN
(*Leisure Hour* 1855)

balance a gain, for it involved a recognition that even private health is a matter for public concern. Sanitary legislation was passed periodically from 1848 onwards, covering matters ranging from common lodging houses to washhouses, open drains to metropolitan interment. Here, as elsewhere, the man in the street was willing to resign to the community jurisdiction over a large area of his life.

The first line of defence, then as now, was the family doctor. But his services were a luxury which the poorer classes could afford only in extreme cases—if then. For the most part they were dependent on clinics and hospitals maintained by voluntary subscriptions.

Despite all the efforts of the doctors, 3 out of 20 babies failed to survive to their first birthday, many more died subsequently from childhood diseases. Children were brought up to accept that from one day to the next any member of the family might be 'taken away'. A children's picture-book of the 1880s, F L Weatherly's *Out of town*, includes these lines:

> *Ah, little one, with us 'tis so,*
> *We know that soon we all must go;*
> *And so we wonder, whispering low,*
> *'Whose turn next?'*

Hospital conditions had been scandalous earlier in the century. More enlightened attitudes gradually supervened, though the initiative for them came less from the medical establishment than from individuals like Florence Nightingale, following on her experiences during the Crimean War.

BETHLEHEM HOSPITAL: THE INFIRMARY, MEN'S WARD
(*Illustrated Times* 1861)

A CHOLERA FUNERAL
(*Sunday at Home* 1871)

One of the earliest achievements of sanitary legislation was to establish national and regional Boards of Health. The General Board was set up in 1848 to supervise public health on a national scale. It was at once inundated with work, particularly as a cholera scare broke out during its first year of office; a contemporary journal commented:

While giving the excellent advice to the public of avoiding over-exertion, late hours and excitement, to take meals at regular intervals and preserve a quiet, even frame of mind, they have had little chance of practising what they have so ably advocated, and have been suffering severely in health in consequence.

The size of the problem facing them is suggested in the report submitted by Edwin Chadwick, one of the Commissioners whose initiative helped bring the Board into being. Comparing the slums of Britain with the appalling prison conditions which John Howard had brought to public attention in the 18th century, Chadwick wrote, 'More filth, worse physical suffering and moral disorder than Howard describes are to be found amongst the cellar populations of the working classes of Liverpool, Manchester or Leeds, and in large portions of the Metropolis.' One of the first tasks was to oblige local authorities to build proper sewers; gradually, as the second half of the century progressed, the open drain and the foetid cesspool became things of the past.

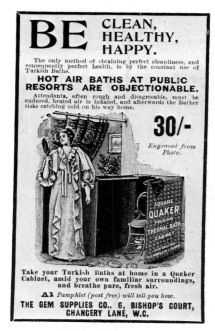

TURKISH BATH AT HOME
(*Advertisement* 1900)

TENNIS AT HOME
(*Girl's Own Paper* 1880)

• The efforts of the Health Boards were directed, first, to improve general sanitary conditions, and second, to combat specific diseases. One of the greatest victories was over smallpox, formerly among the most prevalent of all diseases: it was virtually eliminated thanks to the enforcement of compulsory vaccination, though this encountered considerable opposition from those who believed that everyone has a right to die as he pleases.

Once the public at large had come to realise that health can be improved by personal habits, fresh air and exercise became an integral part of the British way of life. Bedroom windows were left open all night in all seasons, family walks became a regular custom, games in the open air were introduced into school curricula, gymnasiums were attached to educational institutions. Personal hygiene received an attention it had not known since Roman times, though not everyone went to the extent of setting up a Turkish bath in their own home.

Sea-water had been credited with almost magical properties for many decades— whether bathed in or actually drunk. The seaside holiday, conferring health benefits while providing delightful opportunities for flirtation and other advantages, became an annual event for all who could afford it. Nude bathing for women disappeared early in the reign, though the formal bathing dress was a late invention. Men, on the other hand, habitually bathed nude even in mixed company till towards the end of the century— a curate in 1874 was infuriated to find that at Shanklin, I.O.W., 'one has to adopt the detestable habit of bathing in drawers. If ladies don't like to see men naked, why don't they keep away from the sight?' (*Kilvert's Diary*)

Sooner or later, despite gymnastics and sea-bathing, despite the Board of Health, death appeared on the scene. A decent sending-off was desired by all. The more pomp and circumstance the better, as though by saving up enough money for the hired mutes and plumed hearse, the gilded beknobbed coffin and the lavish refreshments, some kind of victory had been won. Strict rules of etiquette governed every aspect of the obsequies; even in death, fashion had to be taken into account. A workhouse funeral, on the other hand, or 'death on the parish', was a sign of failure, on the part both of the deceased and of his surviving relatives, and a cause for eternal shame.

NEW MOURNING GOWNS
(*Girl's Own Paper* 1887)

A FUNERAL
(Gilbert *City Scenes* c1842)

Chapter Nine

Right And Wrong

THE question of what is right conduct and what is wrong depends so much on the individual viewpoint that to speak of moral progress during the Victorian age is to tread on very controversial ground. But one fact seems inarguable—more than any previous society in history, the Victorians were apt to base their religious and moral position on reason rather than blind faith.

Indeed they had little choice. Theirs was an age of enormous intellectual strides, many of which trampled violently on old beliefs. Between 1840 and 1900 the thinking Victorian had somehow to come to terms with mind-blowing concepts in evolutionary physiology, geology, psychology, sociology and anthropology, not to mention new and broader views of history and philosophy. He could either deny such challenges or adapt to them: generally he adapted, trimming his religious principles as best he could.

In some cases, no amount of trimming could square his new knowledge with his old beliefs; he had to let faith go altogether. Of those who managed to hold on to their faith, some swung to extremes—either taking the path to Rome, or defending the extreme Protestant position with bigoted obstinacy. By and large, however, the trend was towards a wider and more humanist view of what religion and morals were all about. Greater tolerance and deeper understanding were the order of the day, and the religious bickering of the period—the anti-ritualist demonstrations, the assaults on Salvation Army processions—stand out as isolated instances in an age whose characteristic voice is one of philosophic doubt tempered with a practical optimism. At the end of the period Britain was still nominally a Christian nation; but its Christianity was of a very different brand from that with which it had started out.

As for the interaction of religious belief with moral behaviour, this remained as confused as it has always been. There was crime, of course, and plenty of it. But notions as to what constitutes crime were changing too: more and more, it was understood as offence against society, or against the individual as a member of society. Life was still sacred, with property running a close second, but the measures taken to protect them had less of the old tribal vindictiveness. The scale of penalties, which had been so

THE PUBLIC WORSHIP OF GOD
(*Pearl of Days* 1881)

unjustly weighted in favour of the property-owning classes (as in the notorious Game Laws) were more fairly adjusted, and certain venial crimes—such as not attending church—were erased from the statute-book or merely forgotten.

The growing density of population, with its social pressures and consequent tensions, might have been expected to give an additional stimulus to criminal activity, but it came hand in hand with a greater social awareness, which had the contrary effect. Insofar as statistics mean anything, they point to a steady fall-off in crime throughout the Victorian age: in 1847 there were 21,542 convictions by trial in England and Wales; in 1874 there were half that number; and in 1893 (after which date a different system of classification was adopted) the number was 9,694. Such a decrease, even making allowance for variations in the application of the law, points to a significant development; it suggests that Victorian doubt, puzzled and confused, was nevertheless more morally fruitful than the unreflecting certainty it replaced.

This did not prevent the usual fears that the moral condition of the country was being sapped. Archbishop Benson at one point had to yield to demand from leaders of society for a series of meetings at Lambeth Palace to oppose 'moral rot'. They were filled to overflowing, despite Victoria's disapproval—why, she wanted to know, should people go to religious services except on Sundays?

For the middle and upper classes, attendance once a week at some kind of place of worship was customary. Sincere conviction or social convention? The motivations are impossible to unravel. We know that many Victorians took their churchgoing very seriously: the 'appearances' of a popular preacher were as loudly proclaimed as those of a star actor. But the social element in Victorian churchgoing cannot be discounted, if only for the simple reason that it was so very patently a class affair. If you were well-to-do, you almost certainly supported the Church of England, that broad and

A VISITING PASTOR
(*Sunday at Home* 1867)

flexible institution which allowed a wide degree of freedom of belief, insisting on conformity only in its outward expression. In the course of the age it was shorn of some of its more blatant temporal trimmings, but retained its anomalous position as custodian of individual souls on the one hand, on the other as adjudicator in moral matters to a nation of which a good part rejected its authority.

The lower middle class, with such of the working classes as worshipped at all, divided their allegiance between the Church of England and the stricter but less 'genteel' non-conforming sects. Entrenched behind a fierce sectarianism inherited from the previous century, less adaptable than the established church, the dissenters found themselves fighting on three fronts—defending their doctrine against rival sects, their simple faith against the new facts of science, and their puritanical ideas of conduct against the new social permissiveness.

The Roman Catholics, a small but coherent minority united by a strong 'party line', drew their support—as a result of historical accident—both from some of the nation's leading aristocrats and some of its poorest workers.

Many churchmen, both Church of England or Dissenting, realised that the churches had to play a new and more active role if they were to justify their place in the life of the community. It was no longer enough simply to promulgate theological doctrine on Sundays and administer the Sacraments as required: the churches must become an indispensable part of the lives of their members. So parsons themselves changed. No longer were they younger sons with good backgrounds and classical educations, on whom were bestowed livings whereby they could lead pleasant, undisturbed lives with a few not too onerous duties. Instead, being a priest became once again a full-time job, whose sphere of responsibility embraced the material as well as the spiritual welfare of his parishioners.

PREACHING IN A PUBLIC HOUSE
(*Quiver* 1891)

AGITATION AGAINST RITUALISM IN THE CHURCH OF ENGLAND
(Cassell's *History of England* 1898)

The great majority of British people were Protestant; and because Britain's break-away from Rome was intimately associated with her rise as an independent nation, there was violent resistance to any suspicion of 'Papal Aggression'. Foxe's *Book of Martyrs*, with vivid illustrations of the Catholic persecutions of Mary Tudor's reign, was accepted Sunday afternoon reading in many household along with the Bible and the *Pilgrim's Progress*. Every concession to the Catholics was bitterly opposed—the appointment of a hierarchy of Catholic bishops in Britain provoked some 6,000 protest meetings and demonstrations. Even the adoption by certain Church of England priests of ritualistic practices which had a Roman flavour to them was seen as a subtle infiltration from the Vatican—and fierce demonstrations followed.

The working classes were indifferent to sectarian disputes; indeed for the most part they were indifferent to religion of any kind. From time to time the churches spared time from their self-appointed task of carrying the Light to the heathen in his blindness, to carry out missionary activities nearer home. Preachers invaded pubs, harangued at street corners, handed out improving moral tracts. But it was the Salvation Army, founded in 1865, which came closest to meeting the true needs of the common people. Its provocative policy during its early years roused considerable hostility, but ultimately the combination of practical aid with evangelical propaganda won recognition and even respect. Spectacular if more short-lived success was also achieved by revivalism on the American model. When the preacher Moody and the singer Sankey opened their London campaign in 1875, 15,000 benighted souls crowded into the Agricultural Hall to hear them.

Divorce provides a demonstration of the confusion between religion and morals which

ASSAULT ON A SALVATION ARMY PROCESSION
(Cassell's *History of England* 1881)

UNDER THE SCAFFOLD, OR THE HANGMAN'S PUPILS
(*Tomahawk* 1867)

bothered the Victorians as it has bothered all societies at all times. Many irrelevant theological arguments were introduced to hamper the path of reform. Nevertheless in 1858 a Divorce Court was instituted as a first step towards a sane solution of the problem of unsuccessful marriages; by 1867 1,279 marriages had been dissolved and 213 more couples separated. But divorce still carried a social stigma: divorcing couples faced moral obloquy as well as the shame of failure on a personal level, and people of any standing in society, contemplating divorce, had to choose between social ruin— even if they were the innocent party—or putting up with things as they were and so retaining 'honour'.

The Victorians were great crusaders. When they had got hold of a cause, they would fight for it doggedly—Plimsoll for the living conditions of sailors, Shaftesbury for the workings conditions of factory children, Florence Nightingale for better hospital conditions, Stead for child prostitutes. But not every crusader was successful; no crusade can for long succeed if it runs counter to human nature or the spirit of the times. The crusaders against 'sensational' literature could clean up the worst excesses of the pornography trade, but they could not ultimately succeed because humans are naturally interested in scandal and sex. On the other hand, crusaders against public executions

SHOPKEEPER ANNOUNCING SUNDAY CLOSING
(*Weekly Welcome* 1879)

SUNDAY MORNING IN LONDON: WAITING FOR THE PUB TO OPEN
(*Illustrated London News* 1856)

found the tide of public feeling running in their favour; a year after *Tomahawk* published this cartoon, the last public execution in England was held, that of the Fenian conspirator Michael Barrett in 1868. Public interest in hangmen and their work might continue, but at least the thing itself was decently transacted behind prison walls. Hypocrisy— or a civilised attitude? Again, that depends on the individual viewpoint.

Another vexed area was the Sunday opening of museums and shops. On the one hand were the upholders of the Sabbath, determined to protect the Lord's Day from desecration, insisting that Sunday opening denied workers the opportunity to attend their place of worship. On the other hand were those who wanted to give the man in the street some more profitable place to spend his day of rest than the gin palace or public house— which were allowed to open when museums and galleries were not. A great deal of questionable logic was expended on the issue. 'Import the continental Sunday and the door will stand open for every continental vice!' declared *The Pearl of Days* in 1887. Eventually a compromise was reached whereby places of entertainment were allowed to open so long as no admission fee was charged; whereafter the English Sunday became a shade less dreary.

The two great social evils of Victorian Britain were drink and prostitution, particularly as they affected the lower classes who were less able to indulge in their vices behind closed doors. A good many of the upper classes were concerned to save the lower orders from their worser natures; unfortunately there was an equally large number who were

(Left) UP IN THE WORLD; (Right) DOWN ON HER LUCK
(*The Day's Doings* 1871)

SAILORS OF HMS TOPAZE SIGNING THE PLEDGE
(*Sunday at Home* 1881)

happy with things as they were. The advocates of temperance had to combat the publicans' and brewers' lobby: the rescurers of fallen girls were up against not only those who stood to gain from their earnings—including the girls themselves—but also the well-to-do gentlemen who shored up the system by maintaining supplementary establishments. A common streetwalker might not have much of a life, but she could cherish the dream of becoming a 'sporting horsebreaker' whose friend would provide her with a house and a carriage of her own.

As it happened, both problems diminished satisfactorily during the period: to what extent this was due to direct campaigning is impossible to say. The Band of Hope, which boasted 1,414,900 members in 1888, was just one of many associations pledged to temperance: yet one suspects that what solved the drink question was rather the changes in social circumstances. Improved living conditions diminished the attraction of alcohol as a drowner of sorrows: while the availability of alternative places of entertainment made the gin palace relatively less alluring.

Similarly with prostitution; the number of prostitutes in early Victorian London cannot be calculated—figures of up to 120,000 have been authoritatively put up; but there is no question that the number declined steadily during Victoria's reign. Here again we may suppose that as working conditions improved, the temptation to pick up easy money on the pavements grew relatively less attractive.

Then as now, the police were seen as lackeys of the establishment, more concerned to safeguard the interests of the propertied classes than to apprehend wrongdoers and bring them to justice. They were also accused of devoting more time to catching unmuzzled dogs than to protecting the citizen—there were parts of London where the police scarcely dared to venture even in pairs; during crime epidemics like that of Jack the Ripper, the inhabitants of these unpoliced areas formed their own corps of vigilantes. Nevertheless, the amount of crime substantially diminished as the number of police increased (by 1856, every county and borough had its own force; during the following thirty years the London force more than doubled, and others nearly trebled in size). At the end of the century there was hardly anywhere that a citizen could not go in safety.

VIGILANCE COMMITTEE IN THE EAST END
(*Graphic* 1888)

PRISONER CONSULTING HIS SOLICITOR
(*Graphic* 1887)

The social standing of the criminal changed completely during the Victorian period. Like all societies, the Victorians were fascinated by criminals; but they did not—like many societies—make heroes of them. They read avidly of the exploits of Charles Peace, for example, and thrilled at his daring leap from the train in which he was being escorted to prison; but they always depicted him as a brutal, misshapen Caliban-figure, more to be pitied than admired.

The Victorians recognised that crime could be the consequence of character defects or unlucky circumstances, and tried to combine firmness in repressing it with humane treatment of the criminal as an individual. Fairer treatment of the prisoner during the processes of the law was introduced; after conviction, prison conditions were improved in the hope of giving criminals greater self-respect and discouraging relapse. In certain spheres, these hopes were justified; the number of female convicts, in particular, was halved from 1,477 in 1877 to 706 ten years later.

Chapter Ten

Invention And Exploration

THE Victorian was an idealist—but he was also a realist. He was a dreamer—but his favourite dreams were those which could be made true. He was a believer—but he believed most strongly where he could feel solid fact beneath his feet. That way, nobody could make a fool of him; for to a Victorian, the highest praise was that he was nobody's fool.

So the frontiers of knowledge were to be pushed forward in every conceivable direction. Wherever possible, the effort was justified by the potential of practical application. If you wanted a Birmingham manufacturer to subscribe to a University extension, you suggested that its work would help boost his productive power. He might not believe you, but he would pretend to. He would rather the world saw him as a hard-headed businessmen determined to get his money's worth, than as the starry-eyed visionary he—like all his generation—secretly was.

Even when the pursuit of knowledge had no conceivable practical application, it had a positive aim. The Victorian who believed himself to be the heir to all the ages wanted to feel he had the control of his inheritance. Just as the fruits and products of the entire world flowed into his warehouses and museums, so knowledge and wisdom from all ages and all places were garnered in his libraries and laboratories. And where there were gaps, he set about filling them.

If the great explorers had not done most of the work beforehand, there is little doubt that the Victorians would have done it for them. As it was, they had to be content to clear up the odd pockets of unexplored territory still remaining. Africa presented the biggest challenge. Throughout the period, explorers—chiefly British, but including Frenchmen, Belgians and others—penetrated and charted deeper and deeper into the Dark Continent. Today it is fashionable to question their motives: but even if their explorations did eventually pave the way for a colonialism whose benefits to the indigenous population were less apparent than those which accrued to the colonisers, we need not suspect the motives of the pioneers themselves—simple curiosity, simple thirst for knowledge, which if they disguised themselves as missionary zeal or commercial

LIEUTENANT CAMERON ENTERING KASONGO'S MUSSUMOA
(Cameron *Travels in Central Africa* 1875)

SCIENTIFIC CONVERSAZIONE
(William M'Connell, Sala's *Twice round the London Clock* 1858)

ROMAN PAVEMENT IN THE POULTRY
(*Illustrated London News* 1869)

enterprise, did so only because the Victorians were ashamed to be called visionaries. But only the visionary gleam could have spurred them to such achievements. With none of the equipment today's explorers take for granted, with none of the advantages of modern communication, their courage and relentless perseverance are a magnificent demonstration of the Victorian idea in action.

The British Association for the Advancement of Science was founded by Sir David Brewster and fellow-scientists in 1831. Among other activities it held yearly meetings in different parts of the country, visiting local geological and archaeological sites. It was the most prestigious of hundreds of scientific societies which were active throughout the country, whose members—not simply scientists, but enthusiastic amateurs from all walks of life—would 'meet to gloze over curiosities exhibited for their inspection, to shake hands and crack jokes with one another—and to ask questions and to receive answers . . . This meritorious association is perpetually asking questions, and though it often receives insufficient, if not ridiculous answers, yet manages, at the close of every year, to accumulate a highly respectable stock of information on almost every imaginable topic.' (Sala, *Twice round the London Clock*.) There was nothing new in this interest in scientific and antiquarian matters; but what had been carried on in former ages privately by dedicated amateurs like John Aubrey or Horace Walpole became now a group pursuit—and gained impetus in consequence. The reaction of the average man in the street to the discovery of Roman remains in the City of London might be a brief gawping

TESTING A MODEL OF EGERTON'S CHANNEL FERRYBOAT ON THE SERPENTINE
(*Graphic* 1870)

HENSON'S AERIAL STEAM CARRIAGE
(*Illustrated London News* 1843)

before he passed on to the next new discovery; none the less there was built up a sense that each such discovery, each new fragment of knowledge, was part of a heritage which belonged to every citizen.

When it came to putting their newly acquired knowledge to practical use, the Victorians achieved wonders. Up and down the country they were continually testing and trying. It was an age when everything seemed possible—having accomplished so much, what could they not accomplish? Now, for the first time, it was the popular imagination, not that of a few enlightened individuals, which dared to envisage the

94

great triumphs of the future. In popular magazines rather than the notebooks of a Leonardo were adumbrated television, airborne police, the conquest of space, channel bridges. Many of their dreams were realised: many more—like those illustrated here—failed. But if they failed it was through lack of knowledge, not deficiency of imagination.

The basic mapping of the universe had largely been done long before the Victorian age. Technological advances enabled them to carry the work farther, checking, confirming and modifying; but the greatest progress was in interpreting the facts, to gain a more complete picture of the nature of the universe. At the same time, they could begin to contemplate the physical exploration of space. The scientific establishment, predictably, derided the possibility, but the public was not going to be thwarted by the pundits who had proved that human beings could not withstand the excessive speeds of rail travel. They listened eagerly to the prophecies of H G Wells, Jules Verne and other such unprofessionals: this story of space exploration comes from the same family journal as, say, the fishing picture on page 71.

For the time being, the Victorians were prevented from venturing into space by their lack of the requisite technology. But a short cut seemed to be offered by extra-terrestrial contact of a different sort. Sparked off by certain alleged spirit rappings in America, a wave of spiritualism swept across the Atlantic to Europe. Communicating with the spirits of the dead became a parlour craze, to be followed by even more extraordinary phenomena, including spirit photography and all manner of physical and psychical manifestations ranging from the tapping of tambourines by unseen hands to the materialisation of loved ones who had passed beyond.

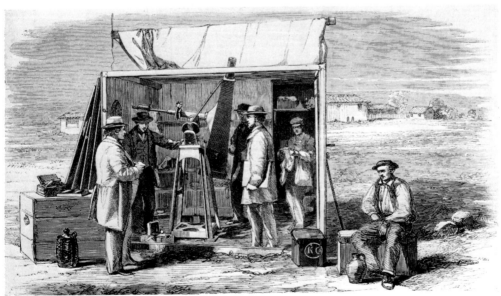

KEW PHOTOHELIOGRAPH AND TEMPORARY OBSERVATORY IN PORTUGAL
(*Illustrated London News* 1860)

95

HOW THE SPIRITS ARE SUMMONED UP
(*Spirit Rapping* 1853)

If such phenomena were genuine, they raised crucial religious and philosophic issues. Many believed in them firmly, and adopted spiritualism as a religion. Others were unconvinced, and because a majority of mediums were proved fraudulent, assumed that the rest must be so too. Between these two extremes were a number who were prepared to take the phenomena seriously while at the same time preserving a healthy scepticism: the Victorian attitude at its best. The Society for Psychical Research was founded in 1882, and dedicated itself to an objective investigation of the phenomena. An eminent scientist, William Crookes, tested the best known of the mediums, D D Home, under fairly stringent conditions, and failed to detect the slightest evidence of deceit. And so the mystery remained, leaving the Victorians as poised between doubt and belief as ever.

Chapter Eleven

Public Affairs

THE Victorian's attitude to public affairs was ambivalent. Broadly speaking, like the majority of people at all times, he was interested in public affairs chiefly as they touched on his private interests: but to say this is merely to beg the question. What *were* his private interests? Not just his pocket, or the security of his family, or the state of his health. There was also pride, local and national; there was a sense of duty towards others less fortunate than himself; there was even a rudimentary sense of belonging to a world community, not simply a limited national entity.

So while he was largely preoccupied with the here-and-now, he was also capable of intermittent responses on a more generous scale; and when this happened, he did not necessarily see eye-to-eye with the professional politicians. In fact, rather than attempt to deduce the Victorian's attitude to public matters from what we know of his nature, it is more enlightening to work the other way round, and, by examining a few manifestations of his latent feelings and beliefs, learn something more about him and the values he lived by.

The new ease of communication undoubtedly strengthened the sense of national unity, but it does not follow that local and regional pride were correspondingly weakened. The great new increase in power vested in local authorities encouraged a new kind of self-respect; every citizen could feel he had a personal hand in municipal undertakings ranging from parks and playgrounds to sewers and street lamps.

Foremost of all expressions of civic pride was the Town Hall. Between 1850 and 1900, municipalities throughout the country—particularly the fast-growing industrial cities of the Midlands and North—treated themselves to palatial new edifices which manifested the pride of the community and cocked a democratic snook at the seats of the aristocracy from whom the Corporation had inherited their power. Stylistically these buildings ranged from the neo-Gothic to the neo-Classical; but in whatever manner they were conceived, grandeur was invariably the effect striven for—and generally achieved, with a panache which might dismay the purist but could not fail to set civic hearts swelling with loyal pride.

97

TOWN HALL, LEEDS
(*Our Own Country* c1870)

The event which best expresses all that we mean by Victorianism is the Great Exhibition of 1851. The fierce opposition which the project encountered from the Establishment, and the spectacular success with which it triumphed none the less, symbolise that victory of the industrious classes over their former leaders which is the central fact of Victorian history. The Crystal Palace was supremely a middle class affair—bourgeois in the best sense of the word—a resounding challenge from the majority which proclaimed that the victories of peace can compare with those of war. The mighty palace was visible proof that the Birmingham brassfounder and the Lancashire cotton-spinner, the Sheffield toolmaker and the Glasgow shipbuilder were contributing at least as much to Britain's greatness as the coroneted duke or bemedalled general. By the time the 6,039,195th visitor had seen all he could digest of the more than 100,000 exhibits, the status of the manufacturer and the artisan was securely established in British society once and for all.

But there were growing pains as the body politic adapted to these internal changes in its structure. There was nothing new, of course, in industrial unrest; and doctrinaire historians can point to Peterloo and the Rebecca Riots earlier in the century, and even the risings of Kett and Cade long before, as manifestations of class awareness and the proletarian principle in action. But the kind of class struggle which showed itself in Britain towards the end of the Victorian age—like its counterparts in France, Germany and the United States—manifested a new and more sophisticated kind of working class

98

THE CRYSTAL PALACE
(Tallis's *History and Description of the Crystal Palace* 1851)

JOHN BURNS ADDRESSING THE DOCKERS
(Hugh Thomson in *Scribner's Magazine* 1892)

SOCIALISM IN A HACKNEY PUB: 'We are sick of being slaves . . . I want a Revolution'
(Fred Barnard in *Harper's Magazine* 1888)

solidarity, which sprang not directly from immediate grievances (most of the workers were infinitely better off than they had been half a century earlier) but from awareness of themselves as a section of society which was not receiving its deserts.

Yet Britain remained a long way aloof from international socialism of the type that was being created on the Continent. J H Rosny, a Frenchman, wrote in 1888:

> *At the present day England, among all the European nations, may be classed as one of the most refractory to socialism . . . Amongst all the British socialists I was struck by their idea of obtaining reforms by reason, by discussion, by a process of evolution, by a conciliation gradually imposed upon the brains of the greatest number.*

Internationalism was not an explicit attitude in Victorian times except among a few exceptionally enlightened people. Those few—typified by such north country radicals as Richard Cobden and John Bright—played a prominent part in international peace movements. By a happy coincidence, a Peace Congress was held in London in the year of the Great Exhibition. The delegates, whose number included, besides many well known names, a party of fifteen French tradesmen whose visit had been financed by Hugo and Lamartine, carried three resolutions which show that some Victorians at least could anticipate the global outlook of our own day. First, governments were asked to recognise 'the imperative necessity of entering upon a system of international disarmament'. Second, 'The right of every state to regulate its own affairs should be held absolute and inviolate.' Third, the Congress expressed 'its strong abhorrence of the system of aggression

100

PEACE CONGRESS AT EXETER HALL
(*Illustrated London News* 1851)

and violence practised by civilised nations upon aboriginal and uncivilised tribes, as leading to incessant and exterminating wars, eminently unfavourable to the true progress of religion, civilisation and commerce'. These high-minded sentiments produced as little in the way of immediate results as such resolutions commonly do. Nevertheless the attitude of mind they represent was to grow in strength in the decades which followed, and eventually crack the rigid moulds of nationalism.

The Victorian man in the street gave a more practical expression of his ability to think internationally when London was visited by the Austrian general Marshal Haynau, who had recently put down a democratic rising in Hungary with extreme cruelty. He was attacked and roughly handled by the workers at Barclays Brewery, and chased through the streets by an angry crowd who called him 'the Austrian butcher'. Conversely, they gave an enthusiastic welcome to Louis Kossuth, the Hungarian leader, when he arrived at Southampton the following year. A few decades later, Turkish oppression of the subject peoples of Armenia and Bulgaria was vehemently denounced by Gladstone, though many of his sympathetic audience can have had little idea where those peoples lived or even what was the colour of their skin.

It is not easy to say with the Victorians where national pride ends and international concern begins. They had progressed beyond the traditional 'My country right or wrong' frame of mind, but in the face of the nationalism rampant almost everywhere in the world, and particularly among their closest European neighbours, they were apt to

101

(Above) GLADSTONE DENOUNCES
TURKISH ATROCITIES IN ARMENIA
(Cassell's *History of England* 1896);
(Right) MEETING OF JINGOES IN THE
GUILDHALL, 1878
(Cassell's *History of England*)

respond with their own brand of patriotic fervour. For the most part it was harmless enough, but many observers were made uneasy by the outbreak of 'Jingoism' which occurred when a European war seemed imminent in 1878. The word was derived from a popular song of the day:

We don't want to fight, but by jingo, if we do,
We've got the ships, we've got the men, we've got the money too.

When diplomacy failed, Victorian Britain went to war readily enough, provided she was convinced her cause was just. Generally she was easily persuaded, though there were occasions—the Opium War in China in the '40s, the Mutiny in India in the '50s, the Maori Wars in New Zealand in the '60s—when thinking people had uneasy doubts. However, once consciences had been taken care of, Britain went marching off to battle with a will; and when she won—which she invariably did—the resulting peace was cause for rejoicing that Right had once again triumphed. Victorian Britain was almost continuously at war in some corner of the world or another, but only once did she fight on European soil, in the Crimea, and in this instance the reasons for her involvement were not conspicuously clear. If the celebratory fireworks were merited by anyone, it was not by the diplomats or generals, but by the common troops who had not only to combat the Russians and their most un-English climate, but also put up with the appalling inefficiency of their own commissariat, which failed to provide suitable clothing, accommodation, food or medical supplies, and somehow to fight and win a war under a supremely erratic amateur generalship.

In the course of the 19th century, the British Empire grew steadily at the rate of 2 acres per second. During the last year of Victoria's reign, a writer in the *Pall Mall Magazine* asked:

How few of that great and motley concourse would say NO to the question, Has your land been the better for British rule? The massed shout YES would go up, and the citizens of the British Empire would enter the twentieth century acclaiming the Queen, shoulder to shoulder.

Wherever and whenever they interfered in the affairs of another country, to fight or to administer, the Victorians believed—and no doubt sincerely—that they were activated by the highest motives, and were carrying out a more or less sacred mission to bring law and order to people who were unable to supply their own. It was difficult for the man in the street back in Britain to know the true state of affairs, particularly before the telegraph had been invented; he had little choice but to take the statesmen's word for it that the people on the spot who were acting in his name knew what was the right thing to do, and were doing it.

When it came to missionary work, the Victorian had no doubts: to spread the Word

FLOGGING A SUDANESE VILLAGER FOR ASSAULTING BRITISH SOLDIERS
(*Graphic* 1885)

MISSIONARIES TEACHING IN NYASSA
(*Graphic* 1889)

103

RODERICK MACLEAN'S ATTACK ON QUEEN VICTORIA
(*Graphic* 1882)

of God was plainly a sacred duty. But the missionary, sent out as he was by the voluntary subscriptions of middle class religious groups, approached the benighted native with a somewhat different attitude from that of the emissaries of the Establishment. A good many soldiers and administrators held the traditional view that the natives were best kept in a state of blissful ignorance, on the same grounds as diehards in 1870 opposed the provision of education for all in Britain, as tending to discontent and insubordination. The missionary did not always prevail, but it is his enlightened view, that teaching must go hand in hand with preaching and even precede it, which represents the Victorian spirit at its best.

There was one aspect of public affairs which passed through many fluctuating phases: the public's attitude towards the monarchy. It was made more complicated by the fact that Victoria lived for so long, eventually taking on the character of a national institution. Her conduct was probably more criticised than that of any other sovereign; yet she was almost certainly more sincerely admired and respected. After the events of 1871 in France, the intelligent and informed Joseph Chamberlain wrote to a friend that he expected to see a republic in Britain in his lifetime. Another contemporary calculation was that one Briton in three favoured a republic. Perhaps if Victoria had died earlier it would have turned out so: but few could contemplate dislodging the old lady while she lived except a few individual fanatics, who made periodic attempts to assassinate her. The general feeling was of respect: and at the Jubilee celebrations of 1887 and 1897, that respect was expressed in a wave of national enthusiasm.

Chapter Twelve

Epilogue

'It is a time of rapid progress, and rapid progress in itself is a good.'
(Gladstone 1879)

WHEN we consider the Victorian age as a whole, by far the most prominent characteristic is change—change in every sphere of life, material change, social change, intellectual change, spiritual change. There have been moments in the history of the human race when more apocalyptic upheavals occurred; but never in so comparatively brief a period has change affected so many people in so many ways. And it is in considering these changes that we find the vital clue to what made the Victorians such a remarkable people.

They themselves considered they were remarkable, and they were right. Not every change that took place in their era can be laid to their credit. Some were the result of historical process: thus, no conscious effort could have initiated the shift of power from the upper to the middle classes—and once initiated, no conscious effort could have halted it. But for other changes, perhaps the greater number, they *were* responsible. And responsible in a new way and to a unique degree. For it was the new self-awareness, self-examination and self-criticism that the Victorians brought to life which gave them the impetus to make so many changes. Less than ever before were those changes due to accidental discovery; more than ever before, to deliberate effort.

The Victorians did not invent the idea of progress, but they were the first to give it practical application on a wide scale; they were the ones who turned it into a conscious process, and made it a mainspring in human life by recognising that in every sphere there is room for further improvement, that every invention is capable of being developed to a state closer to perfection. This attitude can be seen in two lights: as a practical application of Plato's theory of Ideals, an inheritance from the classical education with which so many Victorians began their intellectual lives; or as a gradual approach to divine perfection, derived from their equally traumatic religious tradition. (The Victorians would have been delighted to think that their inspiration came from a combination of Hellenism and Hebraism, to have seen themselves as heirs to the two most potent streams of human thought.)

105

However we trace the origins of the idea of conscious progress, its results are obvious enough. During four centuries of the Roman Empire, the pattern of everyday life scarcely altered: during the six decades of Victoria's reign, it was transformed in every conceivable way. And every change can be related to the ability of the Victorians to examine things as they are—and compare them with what might be.

This is why it is appropriate to end our study with a look at the Victorian at his most outspoken: at the Victorian satirist. Like his fellow-countrymen in all ages, the Victorian was self-conscious about baring his soul in public; but lend him the mask of humour and he became less reticent. The illustrations in the preceding chapters have shown the external side of the Victorian spirit, revealing, true, but not intentionally so. These satirical sketches take us one step closer; here is the Victorian daring to speak his true mind.

Each illustration has been chosen not primarily for its subject-matter, but for the attitude of mind it expresses. Some are confused in aim, some are contradictory, but each represents a facet of Victorian thought or feeling. Unless we remember that the Victorians were capable of such sentiments as these, we shall be doing them less than justice.

IN CHRISTIAN ENGLAND
(*Illustrated Bits* 1885)

(Left) SHORT DRESSES; (Right) LONG HOURS
(*Judy* 1868)

BETWEEN HIS BEST FRIEND AND HIS WORST FOE
(*Judy* 1886)

Self-appointed tyrant, honest dupe or exploited victim—these three views of the working man illustrate the middle class Victorian's misgivings about democracy. The 'honest dupe' image is probably closest to the one most commonly held: 'Vox populi' relates to the riots illustrated in Chapter 1 of this book, and reflects a momentary panic rather than a prevalent attitude. Nevertheless, the fact that the middle classes could unearth such a bogey-man to scare them at moments of crisis is a revelation of the fears latent just below the surface.

107

VOX POPULI
(*Tomahawk* 1867)

108

KING CASH
(*Illustrated Bits* 1885)

Puritanism usually suffers from a deficient sense of humour; most Victorian moral tracts are platitudinous and trite. It is rare to find the puritan conscience speaking out with so bitter a comment as this.

THE 'SILENT HIGHWAY'–MAN
(*Punch* 1858)

The caption relates to the phrase often used about the Thames—'the silent highway'. The river was actually dirtier then than it is today.

(Left) THE SWEET ROSE—ENGLAND 1837 (Right) THE PRICKLY THISTLE—SCOTLAND
1876
(*Edward VII* 1876)

This no-holds-barred attack is from a satire in dramatic form, which advised Victoria to abdicate in favour of her son. Criticism of the Queen was outspoken and often (especially when it concerned her Highland servant John Brown) verging on the libellous.

DIGNITY AND IMPUDENCE
(*Judy* 1885)

The dignified lion and the impudent poodle: the inspiration may be from Landseer's well-known painting, but the sentiment is unfortunately only too characteristic of the Victorian's attitude to foreigners. Britain itself is always represented as a lion, a bulldog, honest John Bull or noble Britannia. France is a beautiful young girl or a contemptible poodle according to the state of our relations; Russia is a malicious but fortunately clumsy bear; America is a rather-too-sharp-for-comfort Uncle Sam, dishonest and devious. If generations of Britons grew up thinking of foreigners in these terms, the cartoonists must carry some part of the blame: the Victorians had many virtues, but tact—particularly with foreigners—was not one of them.

Index